W9-ASO-949

Paintings by RENOIR

Paintings by
RENOIR

February 3 – April 1, 1973

The Art Institute of Chicago

The Art Institute of Chicago

Board of Trustees
Mrs. James W. Alsdorf; James W. Alsdorf; Mrs. Julian Armstrong, Jr.; Edward H. Bennett, Jr.;
Bowen Blair; Mrs. Leigh B. Block; Leigh B. Block; Mrs. Eugene A. Davidson; Wesley M. Dixon, Jr.;
Marshall Field; Stanley M. Freehling; Charles C. Haffner III; William E. Hartmann;
Brooks McCormick; William A. McSwain; Potter Palmer; Bryan S. Reid, Jr.; Edward Byron Smith;
Warner Arms Wick; Payson S. Wild; Arthur MacDougall Wood; William Wood Prince;
Frank H. Woods; George B. Young.

Life Trustees
John Gregg Allerton; Cushman B. Bissell; William McCormick Blair; Avery Brundage;
Frank B. Hubachek; Sigmund W. Kunstadter; Earle Ludgin; Fowler McCormick;
Andrew McNally III; Mrs. C. Phillip Miller; Mrs. Joseph Regenstein.

Ex Officio
Richard J. Daley, Mayor of the City of Chicago; David E. Stahl, Comptroller, City of Chicago;
Daniel J. Shannon, President, Chicago Park District; William Swezenski, Treasurer, Chicago Park
District.

Officers
Leigh B. Block, Chairman; James W. Alsdorf, Vice Chairman; Bowen Blair, Vice Chairman;
Brooks McCormick, Vice Chairman; Bryan S. Reid, Jr., Vice Chairman; George B. Young, Vice
Chairman; Edward Byron Smith, Treasurer; E. Laurence Chalmers, Jr., President; John Maxon,
Vice President for Collections and Exhibitions; S. N. Black, Vice President for Administrative Affairs;
Donald J. Irving, Vice President for Academic Affairs; Louise Lutz, Secretary; Linda Starks, Assistant
Secretary.

President Emeritus: William McCormick Blair.

All rights reserved under International and Pan-American Copyright Conventions. No part of this
book may be reproduced or transmitted in any form or by any means, electronic or mechanical, including
photocopying, recording, or by any information storage and retrieval system, without permission in
writing from the publisher.

Published in the United States by The Art Institute of Chicago, Chicago, Illinois, in conjunction with
a Renoir exhibition at the Institute, February 3 through April 1, 1973.

Library of Congress Catalogue Card Number 72-94956

Design by Graham Johnson/Lund Humphries
Printed in Great Britain by Lund Humphries, Bradford & London

Contents

COLOR PLATES (falling between pages 12–13)

Plate I Return of a Boating Party, 1862
Plate II The Clown, 1868
Plate III Pont-des-Arts, *c.*1868
Plate IV Still Life with Bouquet, 1871
Plate V San Marco, 1881
Plate VI The Daughters of Durand-Ruel, 1882
Plate VII City Dance, 1883
Plate VIII Madame Clapisson, 1883
Plate IX The Afternoon of the Children at Wargemont, 1884
Plate X Villa de la Poste at Cagnes, 1900
Plate XI Ambroise Vollard Dressed as a Toreador, 1917
Plate XII The Concert, 1919

Cover: Girl in a Boat, 1877

Acknowledgement

Special acknowledgements are due the many people who helped in preparing this exhibition. My chief debt is to François Daulte who has gone far beyond courtesy in his help and thoughtful assistance, and without the generous loan of his scholarship this exhibition would never have happened, albeit he must not be held accountable for its lacks. Charles Durand-Ruel has been equally generous and considerate in his help. I am also truly grateful to the kindness of M. and Mme Renoir, especially for their encouragement and their unfailing help in answering my occasionally tedious questions. John Rewald gave invaluable advice when the project was first considered. Equally, I am in the debt of the lenders and their staffs who have been willing to part with their treasures, sometimes at a real sacrifice. I am equally beholden to the staff of the Art Institute, who have been willing to help when it has sometimes not been either convenient or agreeable. I have received this help ungrudgingly, which has solved the many logistical and mechanical problems involved.

J.M.

Foreword

The idea of a show of Renoir paintings was first discussed at a meeting of the Exhibitions Committee of The Art Institute of Chicago in the early part of 1969. Shortly thereafter, it was approved enthusiastically by the Trustees, and Dr Maxon, our Associate Director, was designated to work out the details. Immediately, the assignment looked almost impossible as both the great museums and important collectors alike are more and more reluctant to lend their great works of art for long periods of time.

To do the exhibition alone raises the cost due to the ever-increasing rates on insurance and transportation. Nevertheless, our Trustees – with a strong feeling of obligation to present truly great exhibitions – instructed Dr Maxon to proceed. During the last three years in organizing this exhibit, which involved a great deal of research on his part and numerous trips to Europe and to the East and West in the United States, he only succeeded through his untiring efforts and the great generosity of the lenders. It is with great pleasure that we present to our members and the public of Chicago, and to a greater public as well, this beautiful exhibition of some of the most important paintings by Auguste Renoir.

We are also especially grateful to Francois Daulte, who has prepared two of the essays in the catalogue and without whose advice we could not have done the exhibition; and also to Charles Durand-Ruel and his family, who have been most considerate and helpful. We are particularly pleased at the kindness of Jean Renoir, who has shared with us not only his memories, but also been willing to part with some of his most precious possessions on the occasion of this exhibition.

LEIGH B. BLOCK
Chairman

Cover: Girl in a Boat, 1877. Lent by Mrs. Albert D. Lasker, New York (cat. 22)

Lenders to the Exhibition

Mr. and Mrs. B. E. Bensinger, Chicago; Mr. and Mrs. Sidney F. Brody, Los Angeles; Mr. and Mrs. Maxwell Cummings, Montreal; Dr. and Mrs. Walter Feilchenfeldt, Zurich; Mr. and Mrs. David Lloyd Kreeger, Washington, D.C.; Mrs. Albert D. Lasker, New York; Philip and Janice Levin, New York; Mr. and Mrs. Robert B. Mayer, Winnetka; Henry P. McIlhenny, Philadelphia; Mr. and Mrs. Josef Rosensaft, New York; Mr. and Mrs. R. Meyer de Schauensee, Devon, Pennsylvania; Maurice Stuart, Chicago; Edwin C. Vogel, New York; Mr. and Mrs. Joseph S. Wohl, Lawrence, New York; Seven Private Collectors

The Baltimore Museum of Art; Nationalgalerie, Staatliche Museen, Preussischer Kulturbesitz, Berlin; Museum of Fine Arts, Boston; Albright-Knox Art Gallery, Buffalo; National Museum of Wales, Cardiff; The Cleveland Museum of Art; Wadsworth Atheneum, Hartford; The Museum of Fine Arts, Houston; Nelson Gallery - Atkins Museum, Kansas City; The Armand Hammer Foundation, Los Angeles; The Norton Simon Foundation, Los Angeles; Minneapolis Institute of Arts; The Museum of Modern Art, New York; Chrysler Museum at Norfolk, Virginia; Joslyn Art Museum, Omaha; The National Gallery of Canada, Ottawa; Rijksmuseum Kröller-Müller, Otterlo, The Netherlands; Galerie du Jeu de Paume et de l'Orangerie, Musée du Louvre, Paris; Philadelphia Museum of Art; Museum of Art, Carnegie Institute, Pittsburgh; Portland Art Museum, Oregon; Museum of Art, Rhode Island School of Design, Providence; The Virginia Museum of Fine Arts, Richmond; The St. Louis Art Museum; M. H. de Young Memorial Museum - California Palace of the Legion of Honor, San Francisco; Nationalmuseum, Stockholm, Sweden; The Toledo Museum of Art, Ohio; Art Gallery of Ontario, Toronto; Norton Gallery and School of Art, West Palm Beach, Florida; Sterling and Francine Clark Art Institute, Williamstown, Massachusetts

Durand-Ruel, Paris; Sam Salz, New York

Errata

p. 10, line 13: for ne vient, read *me vient*

p. 26, line 29 and following: for (No. 64) read *(No. 65)*; for (No. 71) read *(No. 72)*; for (No. 72) read *(No. 73)*; for Nos. 63 and 64 read *Nos. 63 and 65*; for (No. 75) read *(No. 76)*; for (No. 74) read *(No. 75)*

p. 27, line 4 and following: for (No. 80) read *(No. 81)*; for (No. 79) read *(No. 80)*; for (No. 79) read *(No. 80)*; for (Nos. 83 and 84) read *(Nos. 84 and 85)*; for (No. 86) read *(No. 87)*; for (No. 85) read *(No. 86)*; for (No. 88) read *(No. 89)*; for (No. 87) read *(No. 88)*

p. 212, No. 6: for yellow, dark, foliage, read *yellow, dark, hat*

Please Note:

No. 52 *Madame Renoir with Pierre,* 1886 (D496) has been withdrawn from the exhibition.

No. 65 *Mademoiselle Lerolle Sewing,* 1896 is lent by Sam Salz, New York.

Catalogue entries are by John Maxon.

About the Exhibition in Chicago in 1973

by Jean Renoir

For me, walking through the galleries the Art Institute of Chicago has dedicated to my father brings back memories of my family. There I find again not only the colors and shapes of my childhood, but a certain peace which Renoir's works offer so generously to those who take the trouble to look at them.

The Renoir exhibition of 1973 will be perhaps the last opportunity given us to explore the different aspects of my father's paintings. Indeed, the value of pictures having risen considerably, the cost of insurance for the shipment of works of art has become prohibitive. From now on, art will travel less and less, and, in turn connoisseurs will have to travel more and more. This will mark the end of great retrospective exhibitions.

When I try to define what seems to me the essential characteristic of Renoir's work, it is the idea of abundance which come forcibly to my mind.

This exhibition will pay homage to true richness, richness of forms, richness of colors, richness of thought. A critic, admiring the work of a celebrated painter of the time, expressed his feelings by saying, "He has painted the poor!" Renoir, irritated, replied, "In painting, there is no poverty!" Not that he denied poverty, for he had known it himself. But he knew that a certain monotonous emptiness can exist as well in the privileges vested in those we call the rich. For Renoir, richness could be found in the movements of a laundress, in the chubbiness of an infant in the arms of his mother.

My visits to the Art Institute begin with a conversation with a child who is no other than myself. I am, indeed, the sitter for the painting entitled *Jean Sewing*. Here I am, sewing, head bent over my work, my long red hair falling on my shoulders, absorbed in a task apparently of the greatest importance. On that particular morning, I had been most impossible. I was about six years old; they say that is a difficult age for little boys. The truth is I was so spoiled by my mother and Gabrielle that the least obstacle to my wishes would send me into a rage. That morning, my father said he wished to paint me, and I had greeted his proposal with screams. Why this surprising revolt, no one knew, not even I. I pretended my leg hurt, and to prove it I limped outrageously. Anxious not to distract Renoir in his project, everyone in the household tried to talk me into it. I had a camel I adored – not a real camel, naturally, but a toy camel, the size of a fist – which did not come from Africa, but from the Bazaar of the rue d'Amsterdam, near the Eglise de la Trinité. Gabrielle, between my sobs, suggested to me, "You should sew a dress for your camel. It is cold. Winter is coming. Your camel must have a dress!" The idea enchanted me. I sat across from my father's easel and started to sew. My father, with his customary fear of sharp objects, showed for a while his concern that I might hurt my fingers with the needle, but Gabrielle promised to stay close to me and to prevent any mishaps. Renoir started to paint, repeating, "If one falls on a needle that should enter the eye, one can become blind for the rest of his life!" But my hair that morning reflected the light in such a way that he quickly forgot the danger of sewing needles and lost himself in his dialogue with what he saw.

A propos de l'exposition de Chicago de 1973

par Jean Renoir

Pour moi, une promenade dans les salles que l'Art Institute de Chicago a dédiées à mon père, est une plongée dans les souvenirs de famille: j'y retrouve non seulement les couleurs et les formes qui étaient celles de mes horizons d'enfant, mais la paix que dispensent si généreusement les œuvres de Renoir, à ceux qui veulent bien prendre la peine de les regarder.

L'Exposition de 1973 sera peut-être la dernière occasion de pénétrer les aspects les plus différents de la peinture de mon père. En effet, la valeur des tableaux ayant augmenté dans des proportions considérables, le prix des assurances couvrant le déplacement des œuvres d'art est devenu prohibitif. Désormais, les tableaux voyageront de moins en moins et les amateurs de peinture devront voyager de plus en plus. Ce sera la fin des grandes rétrospectives.

Lorsque j'essaie de définir ce qui me semble la principale caractéristique de Renoir, c'est l'idée de richesse qui ne vient irrésistiblement à l'esprit.

Cette exposition présentera un hommage à la vraie richesse, la richesse des formes, la richesse des couleurs, la richesse de pensée. A un critique qui admirait les travaux d'un peintre alors en renom et qui expliquait son admiration par l'affirmation suivante: "Il a peint des pauvres", Renoir, agacé, répondit: "Il n'y a pas de pauvre en peinture." Non pas qu'il niât la pauvreté. Il l'avait connue lui-même. Il savait d'autre part qu'elle préside aux besognes monotones dévolues aux gens que l'on appelle riches. Pour lui, la richesse se dénichait dans le geste d'une lavandière ou dans les bourrelets des cuisses d'un bébé dans les bras de sa mère.

Mes visites à l'Art Institute débutent par une conversation avec un enfant qui n'est autre que moi-même. Je suis en effet le modèle du tableau intitulé: "Jean cousant". J'y suis en train de coudre, la tête penchée sur mon ouvrage, mes longs cheveux roux tombant sur mes épaules, absorbé dans une besogne apparemment d'un intérêt primordial. Ce matin-là, je m'étais montré insupportable. J'avais environ six ans: on dit que c'est l'âge ingrat pour les garçons. La vérité est que j'étais tellement gâté par ma mère et par Gabrielle, que le moindre obstacle à ma volonté me plongeait dans des accès de rage. Ce matin-là, mon père ayant déclaré qu'il voulait me peindre, j'avais accueilli cette proposition par des hurlements. Pourquoi cette surprenante révolte, nul ne le savait, pas même moi. Je prétendais avoir mal à la jambe et, pour le prouver, je boîtais avec ostentation. Anxieuse de ne pas déranger Renoir dans son projet, toute la maisonnée essayait de me convaincre. J'avais un chameau que j'adorais, pas un vrai chameau, bien sûr, un chameau-jouet, grand comme la main, qui venait, non pas d'Afrique, mais du bazar de la rue d'Amsterdam, près de l'Eglise de la Trinité. Gabrielle, entre deux de mes sanglots, me proposa: "Tu devrais coudre une robe pour ton chameau. Il fait froid. L'hiver va venir. Ton chameau a absolument besoin d'une robe." L'idée m'enchanta. Je m'assis en face du chevalet de mon père et me mis à coudre. Mon père, avec sa crainte habituelle des outils tranchants et piquants, manifesta un instant son inquiétude que je ne me pique les doigts avec l'aiguille, mais Gabrielle promit de rester à côté de moi et d'arrêter tout geste dangereux. Renoir commença à peindre en répétant: "On tombe sur une aiguille qui vous rentre dans l'œil, puis on reste aveugle pour la vie." Mais mes cheveux bénéficiaient, ce matin-là, de certains reflets qui l'intéressaient et il oublia bien vite le danger des aiguilles, pour se perdre dans son dialogue avec le motif.

Plate I   Return of a Boating Party, 1862. Lent by Mr and Mrs Maxwell Cummings, Montreal (cat. 1)

Plate II   The Clown, 1868. Lent by The Rijksmuseum Kröller-Müller, Otterlo, The Netherlands (cat. 5)

Plate III Pont-des-Arts, *c.*1868. Lent by The Norton Simon Foundation, Los Angeles (cat. 6)

Plate IV   Still Life with Bouquet, 1871. Lent by The Museum of Fine Arts, Houston, Robert Lee Blaffer
Memorial Collection. Gift of Mrs Sarah Campbell Blaffer (cat. 9)

Plate V   San Marco, 1881. Lent by the Minneapolis Institute of Arts. The John R. Van Derlip Fund (cat. 35)

Plate VI   The Daughters of Durand-Ruel, 1882. Lent by The Chrysler Museum at Norfolk, Virginia.
Gift of Walter P. Chrysler, Jr (cat. 41)

Plate VII City Dance, 1883.
Lent by Durand-Ruel, Paris
(cat. 43)

Plate VIII   Madame Clapisson, 1883. The Art Institute of Chicago. Mr and Mrs Martin A. Ryerson Collection
(cat. 45)

Plate IX   The Afternoon of the Children at Wargemont, 1884. Lent by Nationalgalerie, Staatliche Museen, Preussischer Kulturbesitz, Berlin (cat. 47)

Plate X   Villa de la Poste at Cagnes, 1900. Lent by Mr and Mrs Josef Rosensaft, New York (cat. 71)

Plate XI   Ambroise Vollard Dressed as a Toreador, 1917. Lent from the Collection of Mr and Mrs B. E. Bensinger, Chicago (cat. 86)

Plate XII   The Concert, 1919. Lent by the Art Gallery of Ontario, Toronto. Gift of Reuben Wells Leonard Estate, 1954 (cat. 88)

Towards the triumph of Classicism
Renoir's "Ingres" Crisis

During the autumn of 1881, Auguste Renoir experienced a deep sense of depression. Tired of Paris and in need of fresh inspiration, the painter of *Déjeuner des Canotiers* suddenly decided at the end of October to leave for Italy. Suffering from a deep moral and artistic crisis he passed through Milan and stopped at Venice, where he painted Saint Mark's and the gondoliers on the Grand Canal. "I did the Doges' Palace from San Giorgio opposite", he wrote to Charles Deudon. "I don't suppose it was ever done before. There were at least six of us queuing up!"

After Venice Renoir went to Florence and stood lost in admiration before Raphael's *Virgin Enthroned* in the Pitti Palace; then he went on to Rome to study the wall paintings in the Farnesina and the *stanze* of the Vatican. On 21st November, 1881, while staying at the Albergo della Trinacria at Naples, he wrote a long letter to Paul Durand-Ruel. His anxiety can be read between the lines: "I am like a schoolboy with a blank page that has to be neatly filled and, bang! there's a blotchy mess. Here I am at forty and still at the blotch stage. I saw the Raphaels in Rome and found them really beautiful. I should have gone long before. Full of knowledge and wisdom. He did not look for the impossible like I do, but it is beautiful. In oil-painting I prefer Ingres, but the simplicity and grandeur of the frescoes are marvellous." In December Renoir visited Calabria, Pompeii and Sorrento. He also went over to Capri and painted several nudes and a masterpiece called *La Baigneuse Blonde*, which he did from a fishing boat in the sunlit bay. On his return from Italy Renoir stopped near Marseilles and spent several days at L'Estaque in the Hotel des Bains. From there he wrote to his agent, Paul Durand-Ruel: "I was at L'Estaque, a small place like Asnières, but by the sea. My word, how beautiful it is, I shall stay for another fortnight. It would be a pity to leave this fine landscape without bringing something home with me and the weather is superb! Spring with soft sunshine and no wind, which is a rare event at Marseilles. What's more I have met Cézanne and we are going to work together." Unfortunately while painting outside Renoir caught flu, which developed into pneumonia.

Nevertheless the soft climate of the Mediterranean speeded his recovery and he was able to return to Paris. Joyfully he came back to his friend Aline Charigot who had been waiting patiently for him. Apparently it was in May 1882 that the painter and the young woman decided to get married. It was also about this time that Renoir did a second version of *La Baigneuse Blonde* for Paul Durand-Ruel (who promptly sold it to Paul Gallimard), followed by the portraits of his five children, Joseph, Charles, Georges, Marie-Thérèse and Jeanne Durand-Ruel. In the autumn Renoir started on two large compositions with the Dance as their theme, the first in the country, the second in town. But he did not finish them till early in 1883.

These different paintings mark the beginning of the "Ingres" period (1882–1887), which Renoir called his "dry" manner. "About 1883 there seemed to be a break in my

Renoir with Mme Renoir, in the studio at Collettes about 1914

work. I had almost finished with impressionism and come to the conclusion that I knew neither how to paint or draw. In short I was stuck, in an impasse." This confession[1] to Vollard whose relationship with Renoir was rather like that of Goethe and Eckermann, is very important. Following his journey to Italy, after he had discovered the antiquities of Naples, the Pompeiian frescoes, and had had time to brood on Cennino Cennini's *Treatise on Painting*, Renoir went through a profound crisis.

Renoir, and this is very significant, realised instinctively that it was dangerous to work outside, *sur le motif*. "Out of doors" he tells us, "there is a much greater variation in the light than in the studio where it is always steady, but you see, outside you are caught by the light; you have no time to think about composition and, another thing, you can't see what you are doing."[2]

Actually to try to capture a moment in the changing conditions of nature is a gamble. The expression of the model changes; the sun turns, clouds pass over and the leaves of the trees rustle. More important though, and Renoir was well aware of it, the obsession with the open-air leads straight to the suppression of form, and drawing. Paradoxically it tends towards inconsistency.

Such were the reasons that decided Renoir to return to the Old Masters and to choose as special mentors in this new apprenticeship the Farnesina Raphael and *La Source* and

[1] Ambroise Vollard, *Renoir*, Paris, 1920, p.135
[2] Ambroise Vollard, *op. cit.*, p.135

14

Portrait de Mme Rivière by Ingres. Spurning everything he had formerly admired Renoir now despised the impressions of atmosphere and sought instead the draughtsman's style and precision. For fear of having allowed facility and grace too much freedom, he now subjected himself to a strict discipline. The two versions of *La Danse* (in the town and in the country), the *Portrait de Madame Clapisson, L'Après-midi des enfants á Wargemont, Jeunes Filles au volant* and, above all, the drawings and sanguines, with all the numerous variations of the *Grandes Baigneuses*, are characteristic of this new style. Now the artist used only a single outline to depict the heavy breast, the slight movement of the hip, the turn of an arm or twist of a moving body. With consummate skill Renoir was able to unite purity with voluptuousness. Careful examination of the many studies for the *Grandes Baigneuses*, which reveal a surprising density and exactness of line, is well worthwhile and helps towards an understanding of the artist's methods. After 1882 Renoir dreamed of a large painting, with several bathers, some seated on the river bank, others standing in the water. He started the picture when he came home from Italy and it was not finished till the spring of 1887 and hung in the Salon of that year. We know that the ensemble was inspired by Girardon's *le Bain de Diane*, the lead bas-relief on the beautiful fountain in the Allée des Marmousets at Versailles. *Les Grandes Baigneuses* was first bought by the portraitist Jacques-Emile Blanche and sold in 1928 to the American painter Carroll S. Tyson who bequeathed it to the Museum of Philadelphia.

In preparation for the final version of *Les Grandes Baigneuses* Renoir painted not only two oil-sketches, but also accumulated many drawings for the composition and sketches of details. Before he started on his immense canvas Renoir made a series of pencil or sanguine drawings in the spirit of his subject. Whether single figures or ensembles, Renoir considered them all essential exercises, a kind of introduction or training for the final work. As he worked Renoir realised that some forms, well suited to a small sheet of paper, could not be adapted to the larger dimensions of a canvas or cartoon. That was why he did not enlarge his sketches on squared paper. Rather than use an artifice of that kind he preferred to make the figures full size from the beginning and then trace them off onto the canvas. That was his method in *Les Grandes Baigneuses* and also in the different versions of *La Maternité* (Mme Renoir and her son, Pierre). Berthe Morisot was very impressed by this way of working. She had paid a visit to Renoir in his studio in the rue Laval on the 1st January 1886 and wrote perceptively in her diary: "Visited Renoir. On his easel a red crayon and chalk drawing of a young woman suckling her child, full of grace and finesse. I expressed my admiration and he showed me a whole series from the same model and almost in the same position. He is an extraordinary draughtsman. It would be interesting for the public to see all these preparatory sketches for a picture, which they imagine the impressionists produce at extreme speed. I do not think there is anything more to be said on the subject of form in drawing. These nude women walking into the sea charm me as much as those of Ingres. The artist tells me that he considers the nude to be an absolutely indispensable art-form."

When his young wife was expecting her first baby Renoir began to look for a more comfortable place to live and in the autumn of 1883 rented a studio and a separate apartment. The former was situated at No. 37 rue Laval, now rue Victor Massé, and the

Gabrielle and Claude Renoir 'Coco,' in Renoir's studio, about 1910

latter – four rooms and a kitchen – No. 18, rue Houdon. There on the 21st March 1885 the artist's eldest son, Pierre Renoir, was born. Henceforward Renoir devoted himself to family life and limited his horizon more and more to his home. Jean Renoir writes about his father: "More important I think than theories was Renoir's change from the bachelor state to that of a married man. The restless artist, unsettled, always ready to jump into a train to observe the misty light of Guernsey, or to forget his cares in the rose-coloured reflections of Blida, had forgotten, since he left the rue des Gravilliers, what home meant. And there he was settled in an apartment with a wife; meals at fixed times, the bed made and his socks darned. And to all those benefits he was soon to have the joy of a child. My brother Pierre's birth must have been the greatest revelation in Renoir's life. Theories in *La Nouvelle-Athènes* were superseded by the creases in the legs of a new-born baby."[3]

The different versions of *La Maternité*, dating from 1885 to 1886 exemplify Renoir's new orientation towards his art. With an incomparable and natural charm the artist was able to depict his wife Aline, dressed in an ample blue skirt and wearing a straw hat, as she fed her son Pierre on a bench in the garden at Essoyes. Everything here is full, rounded. The mother and child like blades of corn, ripe, heavy fruit in the summer sun. Renoir was so much attached to this set of paintings, pastels, sanguines and black chalk drawings, consecrated to Aline's first motherhood, that in 1916, thirty years later,

[3] Jean Renoir, *Renoir*, Paris. 1962, p.243

16

he asked his sculptor, Richard Guino, under his guidance to make him a portrait model on the same theme.

Renoir, whilst still retaining his sense of mass and ample form, rapidly freed himself from the precise and linear "Ingres" style to return to the freedom of color and frenzied inspiration of his youth. After the beginning of his mother-of-pearl period (about 1889) the flowering of this renaissance grows richer. The successive styles in which the artist depicted reality are concisely summed up by one of his finest biographers: "Color, followed by form, then a subtle amalgamation of the two comprise the whole curve of this evolution."[4]

FRANÇOIS DAULTE

[4] Marc Elder, *L'Atelier de Renoir*, Paris, 1931, tome II, p.18.

View of Cagnes from Les Collettes

Renoir in the South of France
The Patriarch of Les Collettes

About 1900, at the very summit of his career and the fulfillment of his art, Renoir was struck down by the cruel rheumatism from which he was never to be free. Gradually the pain stiffened his limbs till he was reduced to an invalid; yet he never stopped painting and drawing. Rather than undergo medical treatment Renoir decided to leave for the south of France and, after staying for a while at Magagnosc and Le Cannet, settled for good at Cagnes in 1903. He rented a roomy apartment for himself and his family in the Maison de la Poste, which is now the town-hall, and remained there for six years.

From his windows Renoir could look out across the city and its immediate surroundings to a distant view and often depicted the houses and lanes of the old town leading to the gentle slope of the hills. Most of these landscapes, and particularly those of Cros-de-Cagnes, are an extraordinary revelation of Renoir's skill in painting the southern light – the marvellous brilliance of the Midi, that country of crystalline, warm colours, intensified by the presence of the nearby sea.

Once settled at Cagnes Renoir never seemed to grow tired of painting the landscapes and flowers and it was at home that he could best satisfy his passion – painting.

Like Fragonard, Tiepolo, or, closer to our time, Pierre Bonnard, Renoir belonged to that group of artists who find such extraordinary beauty near at hand that they never lose their sense of wonder and must transpose onto canvas the joy and pleasure they feel. No one was more sensitive to the atmosphere of his house and surroundings than Renoir. His wife, his three sons, Pierre, Jean and Claude – called Coco – Gabrielle the young peasant from Essoyes, who was so closely bound up with their daily life, were all treasured models, who appear repeatedly in the paintings, sculpture, pastels and red-chalk drawings.

Of all these familiar models, Coco, born on the 4th August, 1901, occupies a special place. Probably Renoir had never experienced the joy of watching the games and smiles of a little boy growing up before. The way the painter captured the soft complexion, long hair and chubby cheeks of his youngest child show us how he handled his model: "My father allowed me to do what I liked", Claude Renoir confided one day to Michel Robida. "Models did not have to sit still and I could run about all over the place. Sometimes I did have to be still for a minute or two. Actually I was really the bad weather model as much as anything. My father had a regular model for his studio, or else he would start on a landscape. But I was more useful for small sketches, barring exceptional subjects, like *The Red Clown*".[1]

Sometimes Renoir would leave his studio and go for a drive in an old victoria with the coachman, Baptistin, to a place called Les Collettes, near Cagnes. He was enchanted by the old trees of this property and the dazzling views over Cap d'Antibes and

[1] Michel Robida, *Renoir – Children*, Lausanne, 1962

the Esterel chain. There in the abandoned garden he would set up his easel. Claude Renoir gives us a vivid description of his mother "taking advantage of a threat hanging over the property of Les Collettes to snatch the chance of being able to buy it. This beautiful domain, it was several hectares in extent, belonged to an old Cagnes family . . . One of Renoir's friends, Ferdinand Deconchy, arrived one day in 1907 to warn my parents that he had heard from the notary that a timber-merchant has bought the rights to the whole olive-grove. Fortunately the man haggled over the price, which enabled my mother to get in first".[2]

As Les Collettes was only an old farm in the olive-grove Renoir had a stone house built with a sitting room and dining room on the ground floor and the bedrooms and a fine north-facing studio above.

Renoir's permanent move to the south is one of the milestones of his life. On the Côte d'Azur Renoir found principally marvellous country, ordered, and at the same time luxuriant. He never grew tired of it. The garden of Les Collettes inspired him to the end of his life.

However, the realisation that in his later life Renoir developed into a child of the south, a Latin painter and painter of the landscape which had made men traditionally assemblers of form, does not really explain his view of the country. The light of the south cannot be expressed in a landscape in the manner of Monet, Sisley or Pissarro. The light sharpens and divides rather than blending objects in a landscape. It tends towards plane and contour. The type of country best suited to the Impressionist style is a country of dappled shadows and soft, rich tones – the Ile de France, the mouth of the Seine, the Channel coast, Holland and even Venice, which lacks the clarity of the Mediterranean. Surely it belongs to places where the humid, ever-changing atmosphere is mysterious, all-enveloping? On the one hand we have the northern painters like Monet and Pissarro, who suggest rather than define an object, on the other Cézanne and Guigou – southern painters for whom construction and contour are the most important aspects. Renoir was one of the first Impressionists but, as is well known, had reacted violently against their style in 1882. In *Baigneuse* (1916), without realising it, the Master of Les Collettes was experimenting with the style he described as "recreating Poussin from nature."

Renoir made another discovery when he went to live on the Mediterranean – the classical antique. The Provençal sky, so reminiscent of Greece, made him feel that he was participating in the myths of the golden age that filled the imagination of the ancient peoples. "What a wonderful people, those Greeks were," he declared once to Joachim Gasquet, the young poet from Aix-en-Provence. "Existence was so blessed that they believed the gods looked for their paradise on earth. Yes, earth was the paradise of the gods . . . that is what I want to paint."[3]

And it is true that in those last years Renoir tried to resuscitate Anacreon's idyllic world and the bucolic scene of Theocritus, by transmitting the serenity and grace of the Olympians to the washerwomen of Cagnes and to Gabrielle, his maidservant.

Of the many mythological themes that attracted the artist, *The Triumph of Venus*, the

[2] Claude Renoir, *En le regardant vivre*, in *Renoir*, Paris, 1970, p.32–33.
[3] Joachim Gasquet, "Le Paradis de Renoir" in *L'Amour de l'Art*, Paris, February, 1921, p.42

Mme Joseph Durand-Ruel and the painter, before her portrait at St-Cloud, 1911

two versions of *The Judgement of Paris* and the large sketches for the Rhône and the Saone are the most outstanding. In these paintings Renoir sought and discovered the ample forms and finely balanced gesture of classical statuary. Apart from the many portraits of his children Renoir, also, after 1907, painted his friends, pupils, the art-critics, dealers and collectors who gather in his house, Les Collettes, or in his apartment in the Boulevard Rochechouart: the wife and children of his surgeon, Dr. Prat; Paul Durand-Ruel; Ambroise Vollard or the two Bernheim-Jeune brothers, Josse and Gaston; the charming Jeanne Baudot, who left the most vivid of memories with the master; and all the collectors – Maurice Gangnat, an industrialist who had retired to the Côte d'Azur or Mme Thurneyssen, married to a wealthy Munich business man, who had discovered a passion for the work of the patriarch of Les Collettes.

But of all these casual models Renoir almost certainly preferred the women of Le Béal, Nice or Menton, whose luminous skin warmed to the light and who came regularly to sit for him either outside or in his studio. Whatever their names, Gabrielle Renard, Madeleine Bruno, Hélène Bellon, Joséphine Gastaud or Andrée Hessling, called Dédé (and who became Jean Renoir's first wife in 1920), they are to be found in numerous pictures of *Baigneuses* and *Lavandières*. The intense colors of these works, harmonies of red and blue, probably represent the culmination of Renoir's studies of the nude. Nothing then seemed rich, sumptuous or vital enough to describe the soft fullness of these triumphant Venuses. Blood must course through their face, arms and hands,

Renoir and his model, 'Dédé',

even though they might look as red as if they had scrubbed too much. "It is so good to paint women's hands" Renoir declared, "hard-working hands."

The First World War suddenly interrupted the quiet, working existence at Les Collettes. Renoir's two elder sons were called-up and sent to the front. After weeks of worry, spent anxiously reading the news, Renoir and his wife heard that both Pierre and Jean had been seriously wounded. Aline went at once to Carcassonne then on to Gérardmer, where the boys were in a hospital. At that time it was a difficult journey across a disrupted France and, although she came home reassured about the condition of her two beloved children, she was worn out and overwhelmed by what she had seen. After a very short time she became very ill and her husband arranged for her to go to hospital in Nice in an attempt to save her life. But her health had been seriously undermined and she died on the 28th June 1915.

Renoir was not to live for very long afterwards. In August 1919 he spent a holiday in Essoyes and then was able to go to Paris for a few weeks. He was overjoyed to see his *Portrait of Mme Georges Charpentier* hanging in the Salle de la Caze in the Louvre. He was received with the greatest reverence and taken through the rooms in a wheelchair, "like a Pope of painting", and he was able to admire in comfort *The Marriage at Cana* hanging on the line. That was the last summer he spent in Paris.

After his return to Cagnes Renoir began to work again but he caught cold while painting in the garden at Les Collettes. On December 1st, 1919, after a sitting with Marcel Gimond, who was modelling a portrait bust, and talking to Ambroise Vollard and Félix Fénéon, art-consultant of the Bernheim-Jeune Gallery, he suddenly began to feel feverish and weak. The loyal Fénéon, who was present at his death, describes how he had begun to paint a small still life – two apples. "Then he felt death approaching. Two doctors came from Nice, Prat, the surgeon and Dr. Duthil, who was still with him at midnight, just two hours before he died. Dr. Duthill had shot a pair of woodcock and had been describing the incident to the dying man. In his fever the birds kept reappearing and, becoming confused with ideas about painting, occupied all his last moments. 'Hand me my palette . . . the two woodcocks . . . turn that one's head to the left . . . give me my palette . . . I cannot paint that beak . . . quickly, my paints . . . change the woodcocks round . . .' He died at two in the morning on Wednesday, December 3rd."[4]

FRANÇOIS DAULTE

---

[4] Félix Fénéon, "Les derniers moments de Renoir", in *Bulletin de la Vie artistique*, Paris, 15 December, 1919, p.31

The Exhibition

by John Maxon

Exhibitions have many reasons for being. There are the "serious" ones, arranged as scholarly exercises to answer major questions about major artists (and minor ones, too); there are the ones that ask the first questions and let a generation to come find the answers (one recalls the impact of the exhibition devoted to seventeenth-century Italian painting held fifty years ago, of which not the least consequence is that "baroque" has ceased to be a dirty word). There are also exhibitions devoted to a single artist which unveil (and even peel) him before the viewer's very eyes to reveal unsuspected depths or unexpected shallows (as with Rouault). Then there are exhibitions of works by painters so famous, so familiar, and, often, so great, that these occasions seem pleasantly redundant: after all, what more can possibly be said about van Gogh? (To answer that, quite a lot, as it happens, and it always does happen.) It is this last kind of exhibition which not only is pleasant but also always revealing, merely because there is always more to see, even in the familiar works of a great painter.

This exhibition has been planned to survey the paintings of a very great, very French, artist, who shared with Degas the distinction of being the last old master, the last great painter of the old tradition. It has been planned with full and sad awareness of what could *not* be borrowed: the great *Bathers*, neither version of the *Moulin de la Galette*, nor *The Rowers' Lunch*. Further, it was decided not to show the graphic works (with the single exception of a study for the *Bathers* which, however, is not included in the catalogue), nor yet the sculpture, which is enormously interesting in Renoir's career but which is, after all, basically a footnote, and really a glimpse, faintly seen, of what might have been. What, then, has been gathered together for this occasion is a group of works characteristic of the various phases of the artist's career, chosen either because they are revealing about the mutations of Renoir's career or because they are beautiful – usually both.

A word about the catalogue is in order. Because François Daulte is publishing a complete *catalogue raisonné* of the artist's work, in which all of the material of interest to the professional scholar is to be included (as well as due note to be taken, in appendices, of reviews published during the course of the work's appearance), this catalogue omits matters of history of ownership, appearances in exhibitions, or the record of publications. Useful as this material is, it is silly to try to duplicate the work of the most serious living authority on the painter; nor is the material of especial use to the casual visitor. In the case of Renoir, one is not reconstructing an unknown or forgotten painter. One is, rather, looking at one of the most famous of all painters, and the purpose of this catalogue is to help the visitor *look* and, so, to *see*. It is for this reason that a description of each picture has been provided. There are a number of surprises in the pictures, but such is Renoir's authority that he charms his beholder into failing to notice these surprises, which are either part of his pictorial rhetoric or part of his empirical way of recording what he saw. Put another way, Renoir makes his viewer see things as *he* saw them, and he is so compelling and beguiling, that even an experienced observer can simply miss the sleight of hand.

One of the purposes of the exhibition has been to show how the painter's style evolved, and one of the surprises is that his evolution does not fit cosily into pigeon holes. As these latter are really designed to house pigeons and not to be a suitable framework for describing how an artist thinks over fifty years, the shock is not important. What is important is that, out of a sheerly empirical approach to each painting as a new experience, Renoir achieved many solutions which do *not* follow an orderly progression. They have the disconcerting habit of popping up when unexpected, and concurrently with other solutions, so that to date a picture solely on stylistic evidence is unwise with Renoir. It is not to be implied that there is not ultimately a general trend in his work, but the trend is just that – general – and as Renoir worked for his own pleasure and not for art historians and students yet to come, he did not behave predictably.

M. Daulte lists as numbers 3 and 4 in his *catalogue raisonné* a *Venus and Cupid* done in 1860, and a *Sleeping Bather* of the following year which are in blurred soft focus; indeed the *Venus* already is done in hatching, slashed brushstrokes and highly simplified forms. Both look later in date. One then discovers copies after Rubens, and then finds the *Return of the Boating Party* (No. 1 in this exhibition) and *Mlle Lacaux* (No. 2). These shifts in method are *not*, as it happens, the vagaries and chance turns of a young and un-realized painter, but they show, as does the *Landscape* (No. 3), that each picture gave its own problem for solution, an attitude Renoir never abandoned, and it accounts both for the continuing freshness of his total output and for the fact that his pattern of development is definable only in general terms.

There is a first, relatively realistic vein which owes a considerable amount to the impact of Courbet and Corot and sometimes to that of Diaz, as well. And the impact of hours in the Louvre must always be taken into account. Within this group one finds *The Cabaret of Mère Anthony* (No. 4) and *The Clown* (No. 5), as well as *The Pont-des-Arts* (No. 6), and *The Artist's Father* (No. 7), and one already has the painter into his twenty-ninth year. These canvases represent naturalistic painting insofar as Renoir practised it, and each has strongly arbitrary, non-naturalistic elements.

The portrait of *Mme Stora* (No. 8) marks already a sense of transition in Renoir's discovery and absolute mastery of painting in a heavy and ornamental impasto. But by No. 9, the Houston *Still-life*, or the *Cat on a Blue Cushion* (No. 10), Renoir has entered the world of broken color and the search for light and pursuit of its effects. This search is carried still further in the Toronto landscape (No. 11). Yet the portrait of *Monet Reading* (D87) of 1872, in an American private collection, is a step back towards a more realistic approach, as is the huge *Woman on Horseback* in Hamburg (D94), this latter of 1873. The *Mixed Flowers* (No. 12) of the preceding year owes, at least superficially, more to Courbet than it does to the search for light. Thus, one has in the first ten years of Renoir's painting career the pursuit of sober realism and a search for light, but the sequence is no sequence, for he did not hesitate to shift his manner.

The Seine at Argenteuil of 1873 (No. 13) *is* a full-fledged Impressionist picture, but it is equally a carefully observed realistic work. The method is Impressionist, and its realism is that of which Impressionism was made: a careful rendering of optical phenomena which happen to describe reality. The same may be said of *Madame Henriot* (No. 14), except that Renoir has momentarily, in rendering the subject's head, reverted to his earlier manner. The *Box at the Theatre* (No. 15) is Impressionist in both method and intention and does for indoors, artificial light, what was done for the out-of-doors in *Monet Painting in His Garden* (No. 17) of a year earlier. This is the case with *The Bridge at Chatou* (No. 18), the *Sisley* (No. 16), and the *Self-Portrait* (No. 19), of 1874 and 1875. The *Lady at the Piano* (No. 20) carries the method further, indeed, as far as it could go in terms of a relatively rich impasto. The method is carried even further in the light of Argenteuil in the 1877 *Girl in a Boat* (No. 22), as it does directly to 1880.

In *The Laundress* (No. 31) one sees in the systematized diagonal hatching the beginnings of Renoir's years of crisis and the implications to him of enormous doubts, especially about form and structure. Yet the *Flowers and Cats* (No. 33) or *On the Terrace* (No. 34) of 1881 show no such anxiety, while the fragment from the atelier (D358) of the year before is already in the "dry" style. But Renoir continued in his wettest-looking most Impressionist manner, as in *Venice – Fog* (No. 37). Some inkling of the change is visible in the great *Canoers' Lunch* (D379), but it is really only a hint. *The Afternoon of the Children at Wargemont* (No. 47), of 1884, is for the "dry" style, what the *City Dance* and its pendant (Nos. 43 and 44) are to the high Impressionist manner: the summing up. Yet *Paul Haviland* (No. 48) is mixed between the dry and soft styles. But *The Young Girl* (No. 49), of the same year, epitomizes the dry manner.

The River God (No. 50) is both a return to a softer manner and a giant leap forward from 1885 to twenty or twenty-five years to come. From this point, for at least four years, Renoir varies his style drastically with an alternation between the new manner and the old. From this alternation there emerges still another mode, particularly evident in the *Washerwomen* of 1889, which is the amalgam of the two manners, in terms of a rich but disciplined impasto. In *The Apple-Seller* (No. 57) of the following year the manner even includes the effect of dappled sunlight. But the landscape of the *Place de la Trinité* (No. 62) of 1892 marks a reversion to the high Impressionist manner.

Madame Gallimard (No. 63) of 1892, and *Mademoiselle Lerolle Sewing* (No. 64) mark a *détente*, from which the last manner was to emerge. The final great example of this transitional moment may be seen in the *Reclining Nude* (No. 71) of 1902 or *Claude and Renée* (No. 72) of 1904. These sum up the various phases which have preceded these works, and also Nos. 63 and 64. Had Renoir died at this moment, they would have made a fitting, noble end. But there were greater heights yet to come.

In assessing the works in Renoir's last manner, two things must be recalled. He sometimes reverted to an earlier style as in the *Jean in Hunting Costume* (No. 75) which, though it is in the colors of the last manner, is in the technique of the penultimate style, all suave and resolved. The second thing to recall is that one judges the last manner by the successful works, for there were paintings which are, to one degree or another, less than completely resolved. (Here, one must remember that a number of works survived the painter's death which, had he had the choice, would have joined many drawings and watercolors in the stove.)

The 1908 *Judgment of Paris* (No. 74) is one of the major accomplishments of the last style. Here one has the method applied to mythology, although Renoir really was indifferent to subject matter as such; this one made a peg on which to devise a scheme for rendering nudes as a great Hellenistic relief, or even an image from a Roman sarcophagus. The same is true of *Alexander Thurneyssen as a Shepherd* (No. 80) done three years later. The same method was applicable to ordinary portraiture. With the female Thurneyssens (No. 79) the result is not unlike that of the mythologies – an ornamented, elegant surface, full of lively color and textures. With the portrait of Aline Renoir (No. 79) the result is on a different plane. While the painter has eschewed any trace of sentimentality and has been austere and direct, he was, not unreasonably, incapable of suppressing his feelings about his wife. The resultant canvas is not only one of great beauty but also one of elegiac tenderness, a work which speaks a language of pathos equal to that spoken by Hals and Rembrandt in their portraits of old women.

The great nude studies of 1916 (Nos. 83 and 84) show Renoir again with his favorite subject, working them in terms which arrive at conclusions analogous to Titian's at the same age on the same theme. The last summing up is *The Great Bathers* (No. 86) done a year before the end. Like many truly great works, this is not easy to approach, and it is as demanding of its viewer, as one of Renoir's favorite composers, Bach, is of his hearer in his greatest fugues. Renoir felt, and rightly, that his work was as abstract, in that it was not concerned really with more than patterns. The late Renoir nude pieces are not superficially charming, for they are frequently off-putting in their arbitrariness and austerity. Only when it is realized that the treatment of the subject matter is really the starting point, and that the real topic is surface, color, and form: apropos, woman, to be sure.

The Vollard portrait (No. 85) is in its terms also comparable to the late works of Titian. The performance is heroic at several levels of reference. The *Flowers* (No. 88) shows the last daily moments during which Renoir's eye never failed him, nor at heroic cost, his crippled hands. Most remarkable of all is *The Concert* (No. 87) in which he sums up on a soft note what he did in the grand manner in *The Great Bathers*. The substance of a lifetime and the craft of genius are fully evident here.

One sees, then, a progression of stylistic changes from relative realism, through Impressionism, through an archaizing manner, back to a different Impressionism through a simplification of this last change, into a final heroic style which uses the means, if not the appearance, of all that went before it. It is essential always to remember that Renoir did not follow the progression of change unwaveringly, but this practice is understandable if one always recalls that each canvas meant a new experience for the painter, and each solution to the problems he set himself or the stimuli he received, might be totally new, at least, in context, or they might be utterly familiar. It is also essential to recall that Renoir was *not* an intellectual and that he *was* very intelligent. It is also necessary to keep him firmly fixed in his time, place, and context. His son has noted, in his book about his father, how much of the values of the eighteenth century Renoir always kept, that part of the eighteenth century devoted to common sense and reasonableness. Renoir's art is the triumph of sensibility and common sense and, not least, a sense of beauty, as Santayana put it.

The Paintings

Height precedes width in the listing of the dimensions. The "D" numbers in parentheses come from the first volume of François Daulte, *Auguste Renoir, catalogue raisonné de l'oeuvre peint.* Lausanne, 1971

I Return of a Boating Party, 1862

20 × 24 inches

Lent by Mr and Mrs Maxwell Cummings, Montreal

This, the earliest painting in the exhibition, gives a truly revealing glimpse of the thought processes of a young painter. The picture is plainly designed to be a major production, a true *pièce d'occasion*. In it one finds Renoir coping with the subject which Boudin made peculiarly his own, people at the beach seen in rapidly shifting light. But in this picture Renoir shows that he has also looked carefully at Courbet, and the sense of solid reality is the younger man's tribute to his elder.

It is, perhaps, a bit surprising that it is in his earliest phase that Renoir uses the heaviest and richest impasto. Also, in this painting he is using patches of almost pure color both for decorative and reportorial effect. The effect of quickly altering light is not quite solved here. It was to take Renoir more than a decade before he was to be totally the master of the effects of evanescent light. On the other hand, the picture also demonstrates that Renoir was well aware of Delacroix's contribution to the transformation of nineteenth-century French painting, and that he was not accepting the conventional outlook of the Salon but was motivated by both Delacroix's example as well as by the great Venetians of the sixteenth century.

It is in the actually unresolved aspects of this work that much of its fascination lies, for it clearly reveals parts of the creative process at work in the mind of a young and obviously extremely perceptive man. It was only much later than Renoir was to resolve fully comparable problems which are implicit in this canvas. It is by way of such experiments and discoveries that he quickly discovered his fundamental direction.

See color plate I

I

2 Mademoiselle Romaine Lacaux, 1864 (D12)

$31\frac{7}{8} \times 25\frac{1}{2}$ inches

Lent by the Cleveland Museum of Art. Gift of Hanna Fund

The painter has seated his young model on a rustic chair at an angle. The actual place she occupies is unclear, if only for the bulk of her skirt. But the little girl herself is studied with great care and shown to the viewer in exquisite detail. The effect of the softness of her dress of black *mousseline de soie*, with its braided edges and shiny sash, is contrasted with the softness of her blouse, which by the time of the sitting had become rumpled. A further pleasant touch of girlhood is achieved by the fact that the neckline is askew. The flesh is exquisitely worked with the subtlest play of warm against cool, and both the hands and head are drawn with precision and absolute clarity. Renoir has certainly remembered his observations of Courbet's methods, and the flowers are paralleled in the latter's work. Also reflected from Courbet's practice is the use of red touches in the earrings as well as the flowers on the girl's lap, a use which gives a liveliness to the whole and emphasizes the coolness of the tonality.

If the placement of the figure in space is somewhat uncertain, neither can the viewer be sure of the ambiance. It is not clear just what the curtain reveals. Is it a view through a window or a glimpse into the next room? Here the painter follows an old tradition which goes back in time to the sixteenth century.

2

3 Landscape, 1865

$22\frac{1}{2} \times 32\frac{1}{2}$ inches

Lent by a Private Collector

This early landscape shows the strong influence of Courbet upon the young Renoir as well as that of certain phases of both Corot and Daubigny. But this canvas is in no sense a pastiche of his elders' style or manner of pictorial thinking. What is visible are lessons absorbed from other men, but so transformed that Renoir's own intensely personal vision is already clearly noticeable.

As in the case with the painter's earliest works, the paint surface is fairly heavy, firm in impasto, not done in translucent paint. It is as though Renoir was still thinking in terms of the methods he had learned in Gleyre's studio and that his own characteristic concept of paint as an almost matter of superimposed washes or stains of thin but rich pigment laid on in veils had not yet become his vehicle of expression. In other ways, the picture is, for Renoir, a conventional piece of imagery; not that Renoir was ever in any sense a real revolutionary, for he was always artistically in the main stream at heart. But his conservatism was one of spirit and perception, ordinarily expressed in his own idiom. In this lovely canvas the beholder sees the young man at work as he sees the landscape for himself in terms of his own concept of light and color. No Courbet, however pastel in tonality, was ever this blond or tinged with so softly glittering a light. Renoir is concerned with the brushwork of his immediate elders and with the paint surface which can be found in contemporaneous works by Manet and Monet.

What the painter has done in this canvas is to render, and render entirely precisely, the three-dimensional forms of the landscape. It is done in terms of a reversed diagonal progression backwards into space, from the rock at the spectator's right, in the very front of the picture, to the great tree which serves as a *répoussoir* at the left, back along the water-bank to the great tree on the right, to recede finally into the glade at the right center of the canvas. Peculiarly Renoir's own is the pervasive sense of light to illuminate the landscape and reveal its color. But in this picture, as he was to do in the *Antibes* of more than a quarter of a century later, the painter has painted his foliage at full intensity and saturation of hue, even in brilliant sunlight. It was Monet's discovery and optical observation that the purest and most intense hues can be used to render the diminished intensity of color as seen in full sunlight. Renoir, characteristically, has chosen to ignore this observation and create, instead, his own convention of representation. The result in this work is to open the window on to a summer afternoon in the countryside as one knows it to be but does not actually quite see it.

3

4 Mère Anthony's Cabaret, 1866 (D20)

$76\frac{3}{4} \times 51\frac{3}{8}$ inches

Lent by The National Museum, Stockholm

In this very early work the painter treats the spatial structure rather ambivalently, for it is impossible to tell where Renoir saw himself in relation to the structure of the whole. He seems to have been at some distance out from the scene and placed so that his eyes are level with those of the standing, bearded man at the rear of the picture (if, indeed, he is standing). One realizes that the man seated behind the table is at a colossal scale in comparison with the waitress, Nana, the proprietor's daughter. (The standing man at the rear who either rolls a cigarette or is digging for tobacco with his pipe is Monet; the man with crossed arms behind the table is the painter, Jules Le Coeur, and the man in front of the table is Sisley; Toto, the poodle with a wooden leg, is at the very front of the picture, although some distance behind the picture plane; Mère Anthony, herself, is in the far rear with her back set on the diagonal towards the others.) It is characteristic of Renoir that, though he has set his subjects into four planes parallel to the surface of the canvas and has grouped them as well so that the progression begins with Toto to move back diagonally through his seated body to Sisley, then to across the table (also diagonally), to the dishes which Nana is removing, back to the standing Monet, and back again on another diagonal to Mère Anthony, the actual space of the room is highly uncertain. It is so ambiguous that one cannot tell whether the diagonal which cuts the corner of the upper right part of the painting is part of the caricatures on the wall or is an actual beam of the roof.

In the drawing of the figures there is also some ambiguity as to scale, and save for that of Sisley and Mère Anthony, one feels that he has enlarged the heads of the people he portrayed. Yet Renoir's factualism is no clearer shown anywhere than in such details as those of Sisley's carefully observed and placed sandals or straw hat, the china firmly grasped by Nana's reddened and roughened hands, or in the gesture of Monet as he fumbles for his tobacco. Already Nana's head is cast into the rounded form which was to be a hallmark of female heads in Renoir's latest works. There is a curious concentration of gesture and implicit action and relationships which anticipates the same sort of thing in Cézanne's *Cardplayers*.

Renoir already uses a limpidly handled paint with every brushstroke employed to describe his surfaces as he renders them. And each touch makes a delicate pattern in itself.

4

5 The Clown, 1868 (D38)

$76\frac{3}{8} \times 51\frac{3}{8}$ inches

Lent by The Rijksmuseum Kröller-Müller, Otterlo, The Netherlands

This monumentally scaled work shows Renoir at a moment when his style is still relatively unformed, with strong reflexions of both Manet and the early Monet, not to mention the most obvious one of Courbet. In the rather flattened yet pastose handling of the forms of the flesh, there are some reminiscences of the figure pieces of Corot. (It is possible that he was thinking preconsciously of Watteau's *Gilles*.)

What is the most fascinating part of the picture is its stern emphasis upon solid structure, as in that of the clown himself with his fiddle and bow, or upon the structure of the white chair behind him. (The clown-musician was John Price.) The austerity of the drawing (as well as its very excellence) combines with the fluid but controlled application of the paint to achieve one of the painter's most heroic figures. But it is heroism of form that disappears in the particular set of terms seen here, for the handling and application of the paint was to change radically in favor of the more lightly brushed, translucent methods of the phase shortly to come in his work.

Renoir already is using his typical spatial construction with the very high horizon line, and there is an almost brutal insistence upon the flatness of surface within the confines of the picture itself. This is achieved by a relative sharpness of focus in the outlines which insist upon the flatness of pattern. The result is that three-dimensional space is rendered with utmost clarity and conviction, while the drawing and paint-handling emphasize the flatness of the picture plane. At the same time, the use of color emphasizes the sense of light within the circus ring and the lessened intensity of the illumination upon the loges. What was to evolve in Renoir's style is easily visible if this painting and its methods are compared with the *Two Little Circus Girls* (No. 24) of eleven years later. (The most revealing aspects of the stylistic change may be noted in the two hands which hold opera glasses.)

See color plate II

5

6 Pont-des-Arts, c.1868

$24\frac{1}{4} \times 39\frac{1}{2}$ inches

Lent by The Norton Simon Foundation, Los Angeles

The painter here evokes Corot, always one of his favorite masters, in simply applied patches of paint which record a moment of the changing light. Part of his problem is that the act of painting is relatively long and that he was recording a concept as well as a momentary appearance. His problem was further complicated by his desire for an extreme of factual observation in his still relatively somber palette. Where Corot would have sought breadth, Renoir has created color mosaic, a hangover of his observation of Courbet's use of pigment. There is an opacity in the technical handling foreign to Renoir's impulses as a painter. This is one of Renoir's most directly observed and rendered works. Further, unlike many – even most – of them, the paint is relatively thick with almost no use made of the translucence of the medium or of the sense of the white of the canvas visible through the paint layers. It is as direct in its way as any early Monet, yet it has some of the simplifications visible in a Manet. Lovely and carefully observed as the painting is, the effect is achieved through a technique which was not to be long in the painter's repertory of method. A careful examination of the painting shows that the paint patches are indeed translucent, but there is little of Renoir's characteristic pictorial thought. This is closer to the seventeenth century in the sobriety of hue than Renoir was when he consciously evoked the past. Here, the actual colors used are not very different from those used in the seventeenth and eighteenth centuries, and the discipline of the studio tradition is still apparent. Renoir's aim here was advanced for his time, but his means were traditional. In his later work his aim was conservative, but his means were his own.

The picture is carefully put together for both scale and point of view. Unlike many of his works, the horizon line and vanishing point are slightly below the center line of the canvas, and everything is seemingly ordinary and matter of fact. It is only after considering the shadow in the foreground that it must be concluded that the painter either had set up his easel on a higher level than the ground portrayed or else he has adjusted the linear perspective as though he had done so. Further, the two-dimensional pattern is laid out over the horizon line, with the diagonal of the quay set to define to narrow triangles whose apexes mark almost the center of the picture. The shadows at the bottom, offset to the viewer's right, are echoes of the patterns of the clouds at the top of the painting and to his left.

A further nicety and point of elegance in this painting is the fact that in memory it always lingers so as to seem about four times its actual area. It comes as a surprise that it is not a large work. Its relative smallness intensifies the brilliance of the effect which is almost that achieved through the use of a reducing glass. The painting and its limited color scheme is close to the work of Bellotto, for what Renoir has done is to recreate the Venetian's work in the terms of the new pictorial rhetoric of the 1860's.

See color plate III

6

7   The Artist's Father, 1869 (D44)

24 × 18 inches

Lent by The St Louis Art Museum

The portrait of the *Artist's Father* represents a full realization of his technique in oil, and this technique is thoroughly conceived in terms of the nature of oil paint. Yet the tradition of an entirely liquid medium – an inheritance from the china painter's way of thought and working is still plainly visible. Renoir had learned the solid rudiments of his craft from Gleyre, but the previous knowledge of handling watercolor still is visible in the thinner passages of the background and the more transparent scumbles worked over and into the surface of the paint in his face. There is, however, a looseness in the over-all working of the paint, which looseness of method emphasizes the sense of light on the surface of the sitter's face and his clothing. It is not that Renoir does not evoke the solidity of the skull, body, and clothes of his father, for he does, but he is as passionately involved with describing (at even so early a date) the effect of light upon the surface of such flesh and bone. One can see in this picture an awareness of Courbet in the emphasis on solidity *and* surface, yet the suavity and directness of handling and the quiet coloration and play of warm against cool is peculiarly Renoir's own.

Renoir has set his father frontally. The pattern is one emphasized by the irregularity of the visible part of his father's shirt, and the subtle contrast between the cravat and the jacket. But one's gaze is focused on the face, and it is here the play of color is its richest, albeit subdued.

7

8   Madame Stora in Algerian Costume, 1870   (D47)

$33\frac{1}{4} \times 23\frac{1}{2}$ inches

Lent by the M. H. de Young Memorial Museum – California Palace of the Legion of Honor,
San Francisco. Gift of Mr and Mrs Prentis Cobb Hale

Mme Stora, a rug dealer's wife, dressed in Algerian style, repeats the method visible in the portrait of his father, but in this case Renoir has dealt with a far more complex ensemble of costume. But he has carefully emphasized bodily structure, as in, for example, the feeling of the corseted form beneath the bodice of the dress or, especially, in the superb realization of the articulated solid form of the sitter's left hand, wrist, and forearm. Yet this is still a portrait, in spite of the emphasis upon the accoutrements of costume: these accessories are merely bits and pieces of material and stuffs which catch the light and are caught by Renoir in this vein. The rug dealer's wife evokes a Levantine ambiance, but she remains obstinately French.

The canvas appears to have a light toning over the white lead ground, but this may be only discolored varnish which is on the surface of the painting. The impasto is thick, laid down in relative broad and flattened strokes. The colors used are basically blue, gold ochre, red ochre, raw umber, plum, and a few discreet touches of crimson lake. The brush strokes, even though thick ones, are used to indicate the smoothness of the sitter's skin, suppleness and thinness of the satin of the costume, and the sense of the tapestry weave which is parcel to the character of the Khilim rug used, as a curtain, behind the sitter. The miraculous part of the painting is the way in which the forms of the head, hands, and arms are rendered, most especially the sitter's left hand and forearm, which are intensely naturalistic even in terms of the heavy impasto.

8

9   Still Life with Bouquet, 1871

$29\frac{1}{2} \times 23\frac{1}{4}$ inches

Lent by The Museum of Fine Arts Houston, Robert Lee Blaffer Memorial Collection.
Gift of Mrs Sarah Campbell Blaffer

This is one of Renoir's most purely Impressionist canvases. The paint is laid on directly in simple, clear touches. It also is one of the pictures in which he most clearly shows the impact of Delacroix, especially in the use of white, red, yellow, and red ochres, and, especially, crimson lake and raw umber. The particularly fascinating thing is the almost complete absence of blues, the place of which is taken by dull green and, most impressively, ivory black.

The table upon which the still life is arranged is, from the shape of the top, a Louis XV guéridon, which exists only as a shape hidden beneath a glowing, dull yellow cloth. The bouquet of yellow roses (surrounded by lilacs and centered with red roses, nestled in a folded cornucopia of florist's paper) is repeated in size and color by the painted palmetto fan set above the bouquet on the diagonal. The diagonal is emphasized by the frond of grass. The horizontal is reasserted by the print on the wall in its deep-set white mat and black baguette with the closing vertical accent made by the crimson lake ribbon which supports the print.

The painting is one of Renoir's simplest, but subtlest. Its brilliance is equalled by its clarity of structure and limpidity of execution. The technique takes full advantage of the white ground which gleams through the interstices of the brushwork and makes for great liveliness of touch. It is also a demonstration piece of a pictorial method in which the ornament of the actual set-up becomes the ornamentation of the picture surface and of the pictorial space. The painter was to equal the distinction with which the painting is rendered, but he was never to surpass its elegance of concept or execution. Nor was he ever to come so close to Manet in the actual manipulation of paint. This handling was not to be Renoir's characteristic usage, but it illustrates the suavity with which he worked his medium in any vein he chose to mime.

See color plate IV

9

Cat on a Blue Cushion, 1871

$11\frac{1}{4} \times 14\frac{1}{4}$ inches

Lent by a Private Collector

The Impressionists had a way with the portrayal of animals – one recalls the superb puppy in Manet's railway station picture in Washington, not to mention Olympia's black cat. But of the group Renoir seems to have had the greatest affinity for painting cats, especially kittens. This particular cat is really too adolescent to be quite a kitten, but the apparent ease with which Renoir records the bony structure, the flesh, and, above all, the fur and the attendant softness is breath-taking. Only after the kitten is scrutinized does the viewer notice the flounced blue cushion. And the accuracy with which it is all portrayed – the softness of the paws at ease the alertness of the eyes, or the contrasted texture between fur, fabric, shimmering eye, or whisker – makes the viewer realize that the painter's interest is in the effect of light on these surfaces, even though he as a man was susceptible to the charm of youth, whether in human infants or kittens.

The painting is so suavely painted and the image so convincing, that one does not immediately notice the structure of the design both in two and in three dimensions. Again it is a demonstration of how brilliant was Renoir's method, how certain his hand, and sure his taste.

10

11 The Seine at Chatou, 1871

18 × 22 inches

Lent by the Art Gallery of Ontario, Toronto

This landscape is, in its way, one of Renoir's few strictly Impressionist landscapes. The scene is rendered so that the Seine is seen receding rather than on the diagonal, with the near bank to form a *répoussoir* accent. The houses on the far bank are set to describe their forms as they exist in space and as they catch the sunlight from a partially overcast sky. The pictorial space is closed at the center left by the indication of buildings in the far distance, in tones and handling markedly reminiscent of Jongkind.

What is characteristic of Renoir and his way of seeing is the clarity of the paint hues and limpidity of their tones. In addition the touches are neatly and precisely placed with no puddling or smudging of areas or hues except where, as in the distant poplar trees, Renoir is trying to suggest the quality and alteration of color seen in the distance. As the effect of dappled and adjusted light is achieved in a masterly way, the picture is one of the artist's most compelling landscape concepts, even if it is hardly considered typical of the painter's mature view of landscape painting.

In its own set of terms, this landscape is a transitional work in which the painter demonstrates the changes in his own atittude towards the act of painting itself, the fact of seeing, and the interrelation between the two. It was the glory of Impressionism that it stated the immediacy of experience to be a valid motivation for communication and expression. But for Renoir, as for Degas and Cézanne, this was only the starting point.

II

12   Mixed Flowers in a Vase, 1872

$25\frac{1}{2} \times 21\frac{1}{4}$ inches

Lent by the Museum of Fine Arts, Boston. Bequest of John T. Spaulding

The background of this painting is done in mixed areas of burnt and raw umber with a firm but not too heavy impasto. The flowers and fruit are rendered in a heavier impasto with the brushwork emphasized into distinct areas of texture and patterns. These are done in tones of yellow ochre and raw sienna, vermilion (of a rather high intensity), blues, and emerald green. The grey faïence jar is rendered with its ornament done in pure and full-intensity blues, with a secure handling of both the shadows and the reflexions in the glaze. The table top is clearly enough rendered, but there is some ambiguity about its covering.

One of the striking aspects of this picture is its clear and precise definition of forms. These forms are spatially emphasized to the extent that not only is the viewer aware of them but also of the space and light around them. What is less emphasized is the sense of atmosphere. Though clearly an idiosyncratic work of its artist, one can see that he had looked long at both Fantin-Latour as well as Courbet, and he then improved on them. A further bit of the magic Renoir has created in this picture lies in the precise evocation of the species of flowers he is rendering. And while some of the areas covered are almost the same, in size, he has managed to convey most convincingly the mass of the fruit in contrast to the relatively weightlessness of the blossoms.

A further refinement in this painting is the care with which the painter has divided his picture surface into abstract patterns in two dimensions to contrast neatly with the plain surfaces of the background, with the mottled surface of the table top, and the varieties of ornament in the plant material. He has also, in his backward recessions of the flowers, created pockets of space which, in their definition of relative distances, lend a feeling of varied and vast distances which combine to make the feeling of true monumentality in the picture. Actually the painting is not large, but it seems to be huge.

12

13 The Seine at Argenteuil, 1873

$19\frac{3}{4} \times 25\frac{3}{4}$ inches

Lent by the Portland Art Museum, Portland, Oregon

This painting, done at the height of Renoir's Impressionist manner, shows how he differed from his colleagues. For one thing, his use of oil and turpentine as a diluent gives his painting a characteristically rich quality, so that the paint seems to glow from within and lets the white of the canvas be a factor. Beneath the present varnish, it is possible to see that Renoir has diminished the intensity of his colors, though they are still varied and contrasted warm against cool, and they work to reinforce the effect of brilliant sunlight.

The picture is organized into a pattern of light and dark patches set into irregular areas of cobalt blue. The sky is of blue and pinkish touches with a tiny bit of Naples yellow worked into it. The other hues are a dull green, raw sienna, burnt sienna, and an especially transparent black. The few red touches seem to be of Venetian red rather than vermilion.

The pictorial narrative is enhanced by the intensified contrast of the figures in the boat and the dappled reflexions from the underside of the footbridge. This was part of Renoir's version of aërial perspective, so that the foreground objects are in sharper and more intense contrast than those in the rear. The only thing about this picture which is casual is the actual haphazardness of the observed relationships. For the painter had to make adjustments in his recording of closely observed local relationships, and the effect of a unifying light throughout the whole picture forced departures from absolute literalness. But during the time of actual painting, the visual relationships necessarily changed and these changing aspects forced Renoir to make choices in his presentation.

The most impressive factor of this painting is the impact of the two-dimensional design in its extraordinary simplicity. This design coalesces with the three-dimensional reality which is portrayed. In addition, the sense of immediacy is overwhelming, and it is this factor which underlies the spectator's awareness of time and changeability.

13

Parisian Lady, 1874 (D102)

63 × 41½ inches

Lent by the National Museum of Wales, Cardiff

This picture, which is only six years later than the Otterlo *Clown*, shows how rapidly Renoir had altered his methods. Where in the Otterlo canvas the painter laid in his tones solidly and almost without any sense of translucence, he has here brushed and scumbled them so that they possess a diaphanous thinness of quality. The locale is completely disintegrated: while there seem to be traces of an erased drapery, the locale of the figure is now non-existent. The figure is, rather, placed into a kind of fog of warm grey light with the bustled figure softly – even sketchily – painted, albeit with clearly stated details in the dress itself. The attention of the painter, as well as that of his viewer, is firmly focused upon the head of his lovely model. This head and its hat are quite firmly realized with breathtaking clarity and relative sharpness of focus, but without an undue distraction from the whole for the sake of the face.

The subject, the actress Henriette Henriot, who was a favorite model of the painter's, is seen epitomized as a figure of great *chic*, not to say piquant beauty. Unconsciously, one supposes, Renoir has echoed the gesture and pose, albeit at full length, of Rembrandt's great portrait of Jan Six. The gesture is a compelling one, and the figure seen in the act of pulling on a glove always gives a great impression of liveliness and reality of presence. But Renoir has isolated Mme Henriot from the reality and specific quality of a setting, just as Rembrandt did with Burgomaster Six, so that the beholder is forced to concentrate his attention upon the actual reality and physical presence of the subject.

It is only on careful examination that one discovers that the painter has apparently elongated his subject's neck beyond plausibility, or that, as Degas did in his portrait of Désiré Dihau as an oboist of the orchestra of the Opéra, he has sharpened the focus upon the head, while that of the rest of the figure is subtly softened. The result is that the head sits as the most dominating feature of the painting, and one is as conscious of the subject as she seems to have been of herself.

14

15 Box at the Theatre, 1874 (DI 15)

$10\frac{1}{2} \times 8\frac{1}{4}$ inches

Lent by a Private Collector

Renoir used his brother, Edmond, and his model, Nini, "*gueule de raie*," for this picture. Again he has used his customary high vanishing point, this time through one woman's eyes and his brother's mouth. The viewer looks up at Edmond's face, straight at Nini's face, and down at the rest. The color scheme is as sombre as a *grande toilette* at opera is: basically black and white, with a few earthen touches to suggest the crimson and gold of an old-fashioned opera house. After establishing the color of his models' complexions, he has turned his attention to their spatial juxtaposition, and the effect of the two costumes of black and white. The play of color describes the kind of black and white as well as the texture of the costumes. Pale color touches relieve the color scheme and accentuate the play of color within the light and dark. Renoir neatly differentiates between the surfaces of flesh, brocade, velvet, lace, kid, and broadcloth, and lets himself bring glitter through his rendering of the jewelry and the opera glasses.

Technically the picture is built up with a multitude of tiny, caressing brushstrokes which gives the surface a flickering quality, that quality which is acutely the essence of Renoir's first mature style. He has represented the difference of intensity with which the surfaces are illuminated, and as the mind knows that such intensities are variable, the eye accepts the rendering as a bit of illusionistic representation of something really possible only within a time sequence.

15

16   Alfred Sisley, 1874   (DI17)

$25\frac{3}{4} \times 21\frac{3}{8}$ inches

The Art Institute of Chicago. Mr and Mrs Lewis L. Coburn Memorial Collection

This is one of Renoir's most informal portraits, with his subject seated astride a bamboo chair, his arms resting upon the back of the chair. As with the contemporaneous *Self-portrait* in Williamstown (No. 19), the impasto is relatively heavy with the brush touches applied in full, rich blobs of paint. The painter applied a light, rather golden tone over the entire canvas surface as a rubbed-in wash over the surface, but with a considerable amount of the lead white priming still visible. Upon this he built up his picture with direct touches of almost pure color. For instance, in the bamboo chair back it can be seen that the color is applied almost as directly from the tube. What little real mixing there is occurred as the paint was applied. Most of the apparent mixing is optical, with the patches of color set to work one against another to achieve colors seen by the painter and, so, by the viewer.

In this picture Renoir's drawing is at its most "correct" and least stylized for the sake of the pattern of the painting. The informality of the pose, as well as the casual aspect of the sitter, together with the directness of the paint handling and the relative brilliance of the colors used, combine to achieve a sense of utmost immediacy. Because of this immediacy one fails to notice the fact that the scene is in no way determined or described but is really a set piece. The implied window, over and behind Sisley's shoulder, might also be a picture on the wall. (It is, in fact, a rhetorical device taken from early sixteenth-century Italian portraiture in which a window or corner of one is the most common compositional device used by painters.) The only other apparent departure from observed natural appearances lies in the cuff on the sitter's right wrist. As it is rendered, it is ambiguous indeed, and either a cuff-link was undone or else the painter had adjusted the length portrayed, in order to establish the sense of the placement of the hand and the wrist, as they exist behind the top rail of the chair.

17 Monet Painting in his Garden at Argenteuil, *c.*1875 (D131)

18⅜ × 23½ inches

Lent by the Wadsworth Atheneum, Hartford, Connecticut. Bequest of Anne Parrish Titzell

Renoir has organized this canvas in his usual fashion with a high horizon line. What is somewhat unusual is setting a block of space to occupy the entire foreground volume of the painting, one which is defined by the rustic wattle fence set parallel to the plane of the picture. The reality of this void is reinforced in its spaciousness by the placement of Monet's easel, his umbrella, his paint-box, and by the unusual solidity of his body and its position in the pictorial volume it emphasizes. This volume is further reinforced by the pattern of the foliage with its undulating edges on the ground in front of the fence.

The monumentality of the picture is further described by the soaring hedge of variously colored roses in full bloom. The hedge itself has a volume which is meticulously suggested by the placement of the flowers themselves. Beyond the rose hedge a large open space is described, implied by the yellow-green hedge at the right of the canvas and by the soaring tree at the left center of the picture. To the left of the tree, the solid form of a house serves to enclose the whole picture volume at the left of the painting. At the right of the picture, the houses in the distance recede in parallel progression into space and are as neatly and precisely described as though they had been rendered with the help of a *camera obscura.* The final emphasis upon spatial reality is achieved by the cloud patterns which remind the viewer that the sky not only forms a background to the whole but also envelopes the whole and projects to the very front and top edge of the painting, even as it described an infinite distance.

Renoir has here equalled Pissarro at his best and, also Cézanne, in his insistence upon the reality of both the solid and the void, the reality of forms as they exist in space, and as they are so seen. In this picture Renoir also has reacted not only to the reality and beauty of color but also to that of light and the interaction between these two natural phenomena.

17

18   The Bridge at Chatou, 1875

$20\frac{1}{16} \times 25\frac{11}{16}$ inches

Lent by the Sterling and Francine Clark Art Institute, Williamstown, Massachusetts

Even in a subject which he scrutinizes from below, Renoir has used his favorite high horizon line. What one sees first is the patch of greenery in the lower left corner, then the reflexions of the bridge with their pattern rendered in diagonal touches inclined to the upper left. In the middle distance are two rowing figures in a scull, and beyond them are two house boats drawn close to an embankment, which rises sharply upward as it recedes backward. A pattern of houses closes the top of the picture below the sky, broken only by the receding street to the left of center. It is from this opening that the wonderful structure of the bridge is projected. Its solidity is enhanced by the relative clarity of its details and the unclarity of the trees behind it.

Here one sees the painter working in his strongly Impressionist vein. But at no point and in no way does he sacrifice any sense of the solidity of the forms, even though he has softened them in the illuminated, hazy atmosphere. Rather, it is plain that part of the distinction of the painting, the great part, indeed, is in the care and conviction and real success with which Renoir has rendered the relatively vast but precisely measurable space between the viewer (who, incidentally, is imagined at some distance in front of the picture surface) and the large house at the left, set up upon the embankment.

Renoir, quite as much as any painter, was fully aware of the pictorial values of the sense of a large but clearly definable space. He has utilized this awareness to the fullest in this painting. In a very real sense, space (as well as light) is the subject of this painting, and the bridge is merely the identifying and descriptive ornament which alerts the spectator.

18

19 Self-portrait, *c.*1875 (D157)

$15\frac{3}{8} \times 12\frac{1}{2}$ inches

Lent by the Sterling and Francine Clark Art Institute, Williamstown, Massachusetts

This small self-portrait is one of Renoir's most appealing works, one in which one can see the painter at work, as he views himself and his world. He has put himself at right angles to his mirror and turned his head back to glance upwards into the mirror. His head is set at an angle of about forty-five degrees to the axis of his torso, and as he was looking slightly upwards, he looks slightly over the viewer's head.

The brushwork of the head is close indeed to that of the Sisley (No. 18), but the brush-strokes here are drawn to describe the bone structure of the skull, the form and placement of the alertly angled ear, and the textures of hair, moustache, and beard. As the form of the collar and cravat, as well as that of the jacket, are much simpler than that of the head, Renoir has simplified relatively his brushwork in these areas, while that of the background is simpler and thinner still. The emphasis is mainly upon the solidity of the skull with due regard given to the surface textures concerned. As the emphasis is upon form, there is, at the same time, a consequent emphasis upon the space around the head, even though it is in no way described, much less located.

While the brushwork is decorative in itself, its purpose is so thoroughly descriptive, that it does not function with any primarily ornamental purpose. It is this lack of decorative intent which accounts for the fact that there is no emphasis at all apparent upon the flat surface on which the artist worked, a lack of stress which was to be quite rare throughout the painter's career and work. What Renoir has done is obviously to be as direct and straightforward as he could be, in his own representation, and to suppress his natural ornamental bent as much as possible.

19

20 Lady at the Piano, 1876 (D187)

$36\frac{3}{4} \times 29\frac{1}{4}$ inches

The Art Institute of Chicago. Mr and Mrs Martin A. Ryerson Collection

Of Renoir's many treatments of the theme of a woman (or women) at the piano this is, in some aspects, the most dazzlingly painted, insofar as the handling of the paint and colors is concerned. The use of the intensified lead white ground is fully exploited, and the painting is built in myriad, tiny strokes of brilliant color. The final harmony is one of greenish blue and brownish gold with the seated subject of the picture realized almost as an apparition in tones of purest mother-of-pearl. In this painting, Renoir has used perhaps the highest of his vanishing points to give the slightly curious effect that one is observing the scene high above the action, perhaps through a window. (The light in the picture comes from in front, where the spectator is assumed to be.) The still-life of music on top of the piano is carefully planned, as is the placement of that on the music rack, so as to intensify the effect of depth. While the right-hand candle bracket is turned back towards the case of the piano in order, obviously, not to cast a shadow upon the pages of the music, its placement also intensifies the sense of depth in the painting. The whole spatial structure is stopped by the vase with the greens in it, at the very back of the painting, but the back plane remains indefinite, for it is not clear whether the room is closed by a drapery with a golden fringe, beyond which is a glimpse either of another cool room or else the out-of-doors.

Everything is in relatively soft focus, so that the real subject of the painting is the effect of light on a darkened interior. The focus is so soft that one can just make out that the piano stool is apparently upholstered in a flowered wool challis (or, perhaps, silk), and the diaphanous fabric of the dress – *mousseline de soie*, possibly mull – is beautifully realized with its black ribbon banding and blue underdress. It is only after considerable scrutiny that it is to be noticed that the dress is properly a *peignoir*, a note which increases the intimacy of the scene. This touch is the more appealing, for it emphasizes the emphasis upon the effect of light itself rather than on the objects or person portrayed.

20

21   The Garden in the rue Cortot, Montmartre, c.1875   (D193)

$60\frac{1}{2} \times 38\frac{1}{2}$ inches

Lent by the Museum of Art, Carnegie Institute, Pittsburgh, Pennsylvania

The Garden in the rue Cortot, Montmartre is the perfect view from a window. Renoir has pushed the horizon line almost to the top of the canvas. The result is that the sense of space is almost Oriental in that, as objects move away from the beholder, they move up the canvas surface. This is, in fact, what the viewer sees, especially if he not be at too great a height.

Further, as the objects recede into the distance the light-filled air intrudes between the spectator and them so that, in classical aërial perspective, the forms become softer, more blurred. The forms are so blurred as to become, basically, textural contrasts in the painting.

But the real subject of the picture is of the simplest: flowers in a garden in sunlight, with the presence of Renoir's friends, Sisley and Monet, as mere heroically scaled *staffage* figures. In this sense they are no more germane to the total reality of the painting than are the actors in a narrative landscape by Claude. Renoir shrewdly recognized that the real subjects in Claude are light and objects transformed by light. This awareness of his real subject is what makes this seemingly casual corner of garden so breathtaking: Renoir has rendered the forms in and of the garden as they were revealed – even transfigured – by light.

21

22   Girl in a Boat, 1877 (D261)

$28\frac{3}{4} \times 36\frac{3}{8}$ inches

Lent from the Collection of Mrs Albert D. Lasker, New York

In this remarkable work Renoir has an elegantly dressed woman seated in the stern of a boat. Behind her is an oarsman in a single scull, with other craft and bits of the shore seen beyond, at the far (and customarily high horizon) the shoreline. So much for the subject matter which is rendered with Renoir's usual virtuosity and loving care insofar as surfaces of flesh, clothing, and properties are concerned; it is only when one continues to look at the painting that it becomes evident that there are curious departures from reality, so that one is puzzled as to the scale of the seated woman to the craft in which she is put, puzzled as to her anatomical structure in relation to the buttoned cushion, and more puzzled by the relation of the boat to that of the rower behind.

As it happens, the more fundamental subject of the picture is the contrast of the solid and the void, the bulk of the woman on the viewer's right and the intermittently filled space to the left. It is the contrast between nearness and farness, part of the fundamental nature of experience. It is this emphasis upon these two fundamental differences, that between nearness and farness, and the solid and the void, which the painter has employed to suggest by implication the act of motion and, ultimately, the sense of time. The picture, in this matter, recalls the *Flagellation* by Piero at Urbino, which probably Renoir did not know, but one sees a comparable emphasis on a monumental form on the right with subsidiary forms in the distance seen on the left.

In emphasizing some of the painter's traditional problems Renoir is conservative. In rendering form and color, as seen in space and light, he has used the technique of the Impressionists with consummate skill. The most impressive thing about this picture, quite apart from its patent charm and serenity, is the distinction – even genius – with which the painter has combined his flat two-dimensional patterns with the three-dimensional structure he has portrayed, in the seemingly casual, cut-off composition of the motion picture medium. Actually, this resemblance is only a casual one, for the picture is one of Renoir's most monumentally conceived, a painting in which a simple, contemporary moment is transformed into something which recalls some of the rhetorical devices of Veronese. Yet the emphasis upon light, especially reflected light, and the sense of the water and the suggestion of the movement of the flag, is curiously of the time and moment of the picture's painting. Renoir was here both traditional and strictly contemporary.

See color reproduction on cover

22

23 Peonies, 1878

$23\frac{1}{4} \times 19\frac{5}{8}$ inches

Lent from the Collection of Mr and Mrs B. E. Bensinger, Chicago

In contrast to the *Chrysanthemums* of 1882 (No. 39), this is a drawingroom still-life. It is painted in a rich impasto, with the most brilliant of colors, handled like mosaic, with the colors dragged to produce a richly textured surface. The eye level focuses at the picture frame behind the top of the flowers, and the painting of which the bottom fragment is visible seems to be the *Young girl at the piano* (No. 20) in the Art Institute. The vase which holds the peonies is of Japanese style, and dominates the tiny (and unseen) guéridon on which it is set, for another bunch of flowers lies in front of the vase. The wall is a symphony of lavender with rich blues, mauves, and citron tones worked into it. It is not possible to tell if the wall was covered in a watered silk of a mauve cast, or, more probably, if the wall was Renoir's favorite cool grey.

As the picture represents only shallow volume of space, the emphasis is on the ornamentation of the surface of the canvas itself. The painting shows that the artist had much in common with Monet at the same time; but unlike Monet, his aim is more austere and simple, for he has sought to decorate his canvas and render the forms in space with the surrounding air, in a way which parallels that of a sculptor in relief. This picture is well on the way to embodying the relief style of Renoir's last manner, even though there is almost no superficial resemblance. It is the method which is important here, for it indicates how Renoir saw his subject matter, and what his major concerns were. They were typically those of the painter, strictly technical and formal, with any extraneous comment merely implicit in the formal result.

23

24 Two Little Circus Girls, 1879 (D297)

$51\frac{1}{2} \times 38\frac{3}{4}$ inches

The Art Institute of Chicago. Potter Palmer Collection

The subjects of this painting are Francisca and Angelina Wartenberg, who were gymnasts and jugglers for their father, Fernando Wartenberg. They are here seen in the center of their father's circus on the Boulevard Rochechouart in Montmartre. It is useful to compare this picture with the similar one of John Price at the Cirque-d'Hiver of eleven years previous (No. 5). The point of view is essentially the same, and likewise the performers in their milieu. But in eleven years Renoir had softened his touch and had, above all, learned the implication of the softening effects of light seen through a haze. The young performers are rendered in a relatively sharp focus; while the people in the background are in a definitely soft focus. And the tendering of the background figures displays a softness which presages the painter's last manner though without emphasis on solid form seen as a relief.

The paint surface is built of quite thin, relatively translucent touches, with but slight touches of an impasto used to ornament picture surfaces exactly where the ornament is in the costume. The colors are red and yellow ochres, Van Dyck brown, black, cobalt blue, a very few touches of emerald green, a few touches of crimson lake in addition to that in the bands on the front of the loges, and a liberal and inspired use of Naples yellow. There is a subtle differentiation between the ivory color of the girls' complexions, the silver white of their satin costumes, and the pale pink of their tights. The figures are placed in a kind of splendid isolation, and Renoir has let the dark of their hair be an extension of the dark of the spectators' suits. These darks at the top of the canvas are balanced by the rich red-gold of the oranges at the center and the bottom.

While the artist has recorded the effect of the night light very carefully, he has diminished any emphasis upon aërial perspective so that the main figures form an arabesque pattern, and the main emphasis is upon a flat surface of beige, white, black, and gold. The perspective seen from above is especially apposite in this case, and the final effect is one of observing the performers through opera glasses.

24

25 Young Woman Sewing, 1879 (D299)

$24\frac{1}{4} \times 19\frac{7}{8}$ inches

The Art Institute of Chicago. Mr and Mrs Lewis L. Coburn Memorial Collection

This canvas reflects Renoir's accomplished technical maturity. The woman is elegantly drawn with her whole visible body carefully realized and articulated. (Never were hands in the act of sewing more thoughtfully and masterfully achieved.) The painter has used the implied weight of her earring and its verticality in hanging to emphasize the tilt of the head, while the covering surfaces catch the light, as on the inside of the lawn collar or the hair with its ornamental comb. This, the nominal subject, achieved, Renoir then rendered his light-revealed bouquet with the same awareness of form and surface lighted and silhouetted against the window. But there was a new form at work here, for Renoir had discovered Italian frescoes.

25

26 Road at Wargemont, 1879

$31\frac{7}{8} \times 39\frac{3}{8}$ inches

Gift of Edward Drummond Libbey. The Toledo Museum of Art, Toledo, Ohio

The *Road at Wargemont* is an almost perfect example not of water-color rendered in oil, but, rather (by way of the old Limoges point-of-view) of *buon fresco* done in oil. The actual method is not identical, but there are enough practical similarities in the washes of thin oil paint (*essence*) laid on so that the forms and few final passages in impasto emerge limpidly and clearly. Renoir was shrewd in his perception of the means, and in a picture such as this, when not trying for an intensified monumentality, he is suavely, even movingly, not only successful, but great.

This is one of Renoir's most glowing works, in which the technique of using delicately applied transparent touches is exploited to the utmost. The method is the same which Renoir used in *The Wave* (No. 27) of the same year, and it is revealing to see the same method used on two such different subjects. Yet each picture is essentially abstract. The use of the intense, white ground enhances the brilliance and luminous quality of the painting and reveals sharply the precise virtues of the translucent oil medium.

The use of Renoir's customary extremely high horizon (one-fifth of the way from the top in this case) opens and makes possible an intensely realized sense of a panorama. At the lower right of the painting (but set upwards on the diagonal) is the foreground with trees and shrubbery, and this solid is balanced on the left side by a void which is formed by the rapid and sharp slope of the hillside. This hillside slopes down, well below the viewer's point of seeing, and as it recedes to the rear of the space, it moves up the picture plane, where it is finally cut off by the intrusion of the diagonal thrust of a dark blue-green river, the far bank of which is punctuated by the repeated accent of an avenue of trees along the river bank. Beyond this screen, the landscape continues to recede into three separate areas which describe gently rising slopes. The horizon is closed by the top edges of a forest, and there are repetitions of the various foliage patterns in the patterns of the sky.

The picture is one of the most carefully built of Renoir's landscapes with the patterns of nature as seen in the space of the landscape, not only carefully stated specifically and spatially but also as ornaments upon the surface of the canvas. Though the picture is really "naturalistic" in the old sense, it is also almost completely abstract as a piece of decoration. It is one of Renoir's most extraordinary answers to that most classic of a painter's peculiar problems: the reconciliation of the rendering of deep space with the flatness of surface upon which the picture is rendered. It is a brilliant resolution of the problem.

26

27 The Wave, 1879

$35\frac{1}{2} \times 39$ inches

The Art Institute of Chicago. Potter Palmer Collection

This is one of the artist's small handful of pure seascapes. It is also one of his most abstract-seeming paintings in spite of its literal actuality and *reportage*. What one sees at the lower left of the painting is a tiny triangle of sand onto which, and towards which, enough waves are indicated as rolling in. The far distance contains the silhouetted sails of three ships rendered only as tiny triangles. Above these dots, which approach a horizon set at a third of the way from the top edge of the picture, looms the sky, a stormy one, and when the painting was cleaned some years ago the effect of pouring rain from the darkened and lowering storm cloud again became visible.

The subject is uncommon in Renoir's work, and interest lay quite far from such a Turner-esque subject. He has handled it with the greatest distinction, and he has turned the painting into a study of greys, violet, and cobalt blue with accents of white and umbers. A colder picture is hard to imagine, and it is the sense of cold, rain, and chill which surprises. It is exactly a situation in which a rheumatic person feels acutely uncomfortable, and the result is not one to appeal to empathy.

What is perhaps the painting's most impressive quality is its careful and precise coalescence of a deadly accurate presentation – and Renoir convinces one that this is indeed the way the scene was, if only because of the care with which the parts are put together – with an extremely simple and completely effective abstract pattern. If the act of painting, pure and simple, is ever awe-inspiring, it is here, yet in no way has Renoir departed from the appearance of natural phenomena, any more than Monet did in his best pictures of the nymphéas. It is this curious amalgam of amorphous shapes, actual careful drawing, with an intensely personal use of color which makes the picture something that does not photograph or reproduce well but which must be seen in the original.

27

28 The Rowers' Lunch, *c.*1879 (D305)

$21\frac{1}{2} \times 25\frac{3}{4}$ inches

The Art Institute of Chicago. Potter Palmer Collection

This small painting, which is completely achieved and seems far larger than its twenty-one inches of height, is a kind of first idea for the *Lunch of the boating party* in the Phillips Gallery, Washington. That is to say, from such a work as this and *Near the lake* (No. 29), Renoir was to develop his largest picture. This first study of people at their ease at table, under cover, above boats on the water, with the far distance hazily seen at the top, is brilliant in its own right. In some ways it is more appealing than the large picture simply because it is not a tour-de-force.

The color scheme is based on cobalt blue, gold ochre, Naples yellow, red ochre, raw umber, green, and white, with a few touches of carmine, as well as red earth. The brushwork is brilliantly done and captures precisely the effect of real people at ease. The painting contains not only two breath-taking portraits (three if one will include the woman seen from behind) but also a dazzling summer landscape, and one of the loveliest and most economical still-lifes in all of French painting. It is here that the discipline of Gleyre's studio and the methods of Limoges combine to produce a masterpiece. The softness of focus, which is a concomitant of the shaded setting under the trelliswork, is also the technical device to emphasize the heroic concept of this work and to make it transcend its small size.

The forms are placed so that there is not only a rhythmic movement backwards into space but also an emphasis upon their solidity. This has the consequence of making the near space within the pavilion seem larger and more enveloping than it is. Yet the light is so rendered that there is a smooth transition to that of the space outside, with an enveloping limpidity throughout the entire surface of the painting. The brilliance of Renoir's achievement is that one can concentrate upon the bottles, glasses, compotier, and, above all, the nasturtiums, without realizing the finesse with which the painter has produced this gem. Drawing, brushwork, and spatial design, combine with and make a two-dimensional pattern to ornament the surface with dazzling intensity.

29 Near the Lake, *c.*1879 (D306)

18⅛ × 21¾ inches

The Art Institute of Chicago. Potter Palmer Collection

This is almost a pendant to the preceding picture, for it is of the same character and shows a comparable scene. Here one sees the figures, a man in casual attire with a cigarette in his hand (he seems to have been left-handed) relaxed as he leans against a red painted wooden balustrade, and a woman seated facing him, her arms rested on the ledge. The top of the picture is closed by a vine-covered screen, from which vines extend. These figures are painted in brilliant touches of inter-worked blues, reds, umbers, and yellows, done in relatively sharp focus. Beyond them, well below, is a lake with boats and people at its edge. In the far distance is an expanse of grass with indistinct trees to close the view. The sky appears only as a thin band of almost pure white between the canopy and these trees.

The construction is that of pure theatre, with the foreground of vast importance, done as a piece of cut-out sculpture. The distant view is at a seemingly enormous scale merely because so much is shown. What is striking in the painting is the way in which Renoir has managed to adjust his focus on foreground and background to make them equally important. In actuality the whole would never be seen in this way. It is in this adjustment of the focus, as well as of the values, by which he manages to preserve the sense of a flat surface, even though he is rendering solids and space seen in air and light. The effect is indeed magical, but there is not much more which could have been done in this vein, except, perhaps, to systematize the brushwork, which Renoir was to do in *The Laundress* (No. 31), shortly after this painting.

29

30   At the Concert, 1880   (D329)

$39\frac{1}{16} \times 31\frac{3}{4}$ inches

Lent by the Sterling and Francine Clark Art Institute. Williamstown, Massachusetts

Renoir has taken his two elegant subjects (the wife and daughter of the Under-Secretary of the Beaux-Arts, Edmond Turquet) and placed them in a box at the opera. The principal subject is seen half length at her ease on a sofa. She holds some sheets of music in her white-gloved right hand, while her left one supports her chin as she gazes at the beholder head on. Her undergarment appears to be of satin, while the applied overdress is of chiffon, as the embroidered cap sleeves show. In front of her, well to the right, seated on the diagonal, is a much younger woman whose flowing hair is braided with a wide ribbon. This young woman holds a wrapped bouquet of flowers. Together these two figures are the major forms of the painting and define a large volume which recedes diagonally from the lower right to the upper left center. At this point a fluted pilaster is visible above the back of the banquette, and the whole of the remaining rear of the painting is closed by a hanging drapery.

It is a little hard to decide how much of the composition of the painting owes to the traditions of Van Dyck, and the grand manner of the seventeenth century and how much of what is there is simply Renoir's reportage of the scene. As it is, the painting is a superb example of the relaxed style of the painter's first maturity which was to end with his years of crisis. This picture gives a precise set of visual clues to the ultimate causes of the crisis, for there really was nothing further for the painter to do in this manner. Further refinements of surface would have produced increased suavity of finish and decreased vitality in the whole. The painting is as close as Renoir approaches to the feel of the Salon, and though Renoir had a strongly conservative streak in him, he had little of the *Salonnier* in his nature. It is no wonder, then, that he was to develop severe intellectual and emotional doubts about his work. This is implicitly evident in this picture, brilliant as it is.

30

31 The Laundress, *c.*1880 (D348)

$32 \times 22\frac{3}{8}$ inches

The Art Institute of Chicago. Charles H. and Mary F. S. Worcester Collection

The Laundress represents Renoir's awareness of the quality of light, that is, its capacity to draw a scene into a whole, as well as its capacity to reveal specific details. And in this case one can see his closest approach to Pissarro and his methods. Renoir, as a consummate craftsman, worked throughout his career to solve certain technical matters to his own satisfaction. These solutions are the organization and superimposition of the brushstrokes in alternating diagonals, freely done. Renoir here achieves, by reason of his craft and experimentation, some things which Seurat was to do by dint of thought.

The principal pictorial innovation is that it is not only a mosaic of color applied in delicate, pastose touches, it is also an arabesque in which various hues are juxtaposed so that while there are prevailing tonalities, there cannot be said to be prevailing colors. The color patches, such as the rose ones of the face, or the color of the skirt, are all altered by the presence of other hues which serve to modulate any sense of harshness. The main function of these juxta-positions is to enhance the feeling of light and the alterations to observed color under the effect of light.

As far as subject matter goes, and even in the manner of presentation, the painting, although it does not resemble, evokes strongly the bourgeois side of Chardin, not one of Renoir's favorite artists. It is in such a picture as this, which is not really one of the artist's easiest works to understand, that one can feel his innate traditionalism.

31

32 Girl with Falcon, 1880 (D349)

$49 \frac{13}{16} \times 30 \frac{3}{4}$ inches

Lent by the Sterling and Francine Clark Art Institute, Williamstown, Massachusetts

This is an almost too pretty piece of orientalized taste on the painter's part. What saves the painting from any real vulgarity, though, is the fact that not only is the picture beautifully drawn, but it is also beautifully painted. The image of the pretty little girl (a Mlle Fleury) is solidly achieved and extraordinarily cogently observed. One really has in this figure the essence of scrawny girlhood, of which the meagerness is redeemed by the lushness of the costume and the effect of liveliness in her face. It is only after a considerable time that one notices that the floor tiles' pattern seems in ill accord with the doorway. Then one notices that Renoir has used his typical device of the high horizon line, with a vanishing point set well to the right edge of the canvas.

The painting as a whole achieves its success through the distinction of the large patterns formed on its surface and the relief provided by the details of the costume, the features of the child, and the feathers of her bird. A further fillip is given to the picture by the gesture of the little girl who holds the ruffled, patterned curtain aside. This action carries with it the implication of motion and time, and the result is that of a moment stopped, as by a camera flash, which increases the effect of spontaneity and the feeling of the instantaneous, no mean accomplishment, the more so as it is basically alien to the painter's purpose, especially one so classically oriented as Renoir was.

The brilliance of the painting, as well as its rich coloration, reveal what Renoir admired in Delacroix. And the concentration and absolute intensity of the implied simple action evokes, of all people, the example of Liotard. But Renoir is completely himself here, all his influences digested, absorbed, and part of his artistic bloodstream.

32

33 Flowers and Cats, 1881

$36\frac{1}{2} \times 29$ inches

Lent from the Collection of Mrs Albert D. Lasker, New York

This canvas embodies all of Renoir's technical elegance of the opening years of the 'eighties. In it one sees the perfection of his adaptation of his china-painting technique as translated into the oil medium. The paint is used in a way which is strictly consonant with the exigencies of the oil technique, lightened and made luminous beyond mere translucence to the point of apparent (though not real) transparency. The emphasis which Renoir has made of this device and his insistent use of the whiteness of the ground as a constant presence makes the picture technically one of his most brilliant. The painting is suffused with light, yet it is really impossible to determine the source of the light. What occurs is that the forms are revealed by the use of the colors represented. The picture is done in delicate touches which emphasize first, the contrasts between varieties of tawny reds and cool greens, and second, the play of varieties of Naples yellow against blue. The final binding accents are subtle umbers and greys which not only set off the colors, but also define the varieties of whites employed. The entire color harmony emphasizes the sense of light and the reality of luminosity, which is achieved partly through the technical means used in applying the paint (so that the white ground of the canvas remains a pervasive part of the whole), and partly by a careful adjustment of the hues, intensities, and the values and their relationships.

The subject matter is merely a bowl of potted geraniums set into an oriental *cáchepot*, which in its turn is placed upon a matching ceramic stand. Before this bowl, set at an angle to the viewer's right, is seen the corner of a table, of which the carved edge, the supporting frame, and the top of the legs, cut in a solomonic form. Upon this table top is a yarn basket within which and at the edge of which two kittens are playing with the yarn. Below the table and the jardinière the floor of white and grey marble is visible at the viewer's left. Behind all of these solids may be discerned a blue curtain, apparently of velours, and beyond that, but ambiguously rendered, a screen, a bit of a door (?), and the parquet below. As the painting has evolved, the spectator perceives a monumental volume which consists, paradoxically, of the relatively fragile, fractured forms of the geranium blossoms and their leaves, carefully placed upon (rather than into) the volume of the Chinese bowl and its base. The kittens at play with the void of the yarn basket serve to emphasize the great bulk of the flowers, while the diagonal of the table emphasizes the *répoussoir* function of the latter and, in contrast with the orthogonals of the marble floor tiles, emphasizes the sense of space and of complicated forms which exist in space.

There are ambiguities in the painting which, upon consideration, seem hard to explain or reconcile. Just what the velvet curtain conceals is hard to tell, and the spatial structure of the screen is equally indeterminate. Indeed, it may be asked if the golden-red passage at the spectator's left really is a screen or, rather, an incompletely defined curtain. But the most surprising thing about the picture is the curious scale relationship between the bowl of geraniums and its support (in the center of the picture space) and that of the table with yarn basket and the kittens, which latter are ruthlessly reduced in scale. As it happens, these ambiguities of scale are unimportant to the painter's purpose, which seems to have been the establishment of the relatively vast form of the plant and its container as they exist in space and air, with the supporting material in front made subsidiary to the goal.

A further aim of Renoir's in this picture is to ornament the surface of his canvas almost as though it were a porcelain plate. In the doing, he has preserved the paradox of the sense of the flatness of the surface of the canvas as well as the sense of space and air in things represented.

33

Renoir forces his spectator to accept the visual reality as he has rendered it, even though it does not strictly accord with rational experience. He may well have added the table, the yarn basket, and the kittens after he had the jardinière and the geraniums well set upon the canvas. His purpose would have been not only to add simple narrative interest – and Renoir was indeed interested in the life lived around him – but also to emphasize the contrast of the living plants with inanimate forms about them; and the contrast is further emphasized by the suggested movement of the kittens. Pictorially his purpose remains quite plain: to emphasize the monumental form and scale of the plants in their container, and this is achieved by abandoning the ordinary scale relationships of everyday reality. Thus, it can be seen that this seemingly naturalistic painting is, rather, a carefully considered and contrived recreation of visual experience purely into the painter's terms. Renoir has not hesitated to alter ordinary natural experiences to achieve this aim, for not only has he altered visual scale to achieve his purpose, but he has also altered simple orthogonal projection as well, as a glance at the marble pavement proves.

34 On the Terrace, 1881 (D378)

$39\frac{1}{2} \times 31\frac{7}{8}$ inches

The Art Institute of Chicago. Mr and Mrs Lewis L. Coburn Memorial Collection

This famous and immensely popular work of Renoir's early high period is, upon examination, one of his most surprising and curious, for what seems to be a simple, naturalistic painting is no such thing. The woman has a curious anatomical construction with a head too large for her body, and her non-existent rump is placed high into the back of the chair and would, if it existed, impinge on the tub of plants. This latter is grossly overscaled, and the balcony rail runs through its center, then to bend to the left of the seated woman. The child, who would be well under three years of age, is larger in scale than life, and so is the basket of yarn. Insofar as formal structure is concerned, what seems a straightforward natural representation is, in fact, a piece of Mannerist construction, with the space and the forms in it arbitrarily rearranged to suit the painter's purpose. Yet the individual parts are superlatively drawn, and the flesh surfaces, as well as those of the costumes, are brilliantly painted.

The structure of the space is conceived as a set of zig-zag diagonals which, as they recede, describe and contain increasingly large volumes. As the space recedes, the focus of the painting is softened in a fashion which parallels Degas's methods, but in Renoir's own way. The spectator, with the painter, looks down at the subject and out through the trees to the horizon with the house on the far bank and boats between. The focus of the foliage is blurred to force the gaze on the two sitters. The mother and child are rendered so as to capture the full effect of dappled sunlight seen late on a summer afternoon.

The painter has emphasized details of costume and features so thoroughly that the beholder accepts their reality in detail without considering the whole. The woman's folded hands are worthy of Boucher or Fragonard, and those of the child veritably epitomize infancy. The woman's eyes, nose, and partly opened lips mark the center of the canvas and are the focal point of the picture. This and the rest of the local reality are so brilliantly achieved that the viewer accepts the remaining parts of the picture on faith and never notices that they are in most ways as mutually exclusive and improbable as their counterparts in a work by Bronzino or Rosso.

34

35 San Marco, 1881

25 × 32 inches

Lent by the Minneapolis Institute of Arts. The John R. Van Derlip Fund

The painting has the qualities and technique of a sketch. But it is not a sketch. It is the reduction of the scene into patches of relatively brilliant colors – reds, blues, and Naples yellow, with dark umber touches. Renoir has all but ignored the pattern in the pavement of Istrian limestone used by Canaletto (and all since him) to define the measure of the square. He has submerged the great red ochre flag poles, while people have become elongated touches from his brush. The paint is so loosely and unevenly applied that a great amount of the priming is visible. It is almost as if Renoir were translating his view with a mosaic-like pattern in emulation of the mosaics and *pietra-dura* work in front of him. The only other painter who had a roughly comparable reaction to Venice was Turner, who was swamped by the survival of his years in the eighteenth century. But Renoir's invention is his own. He did not care for Turner's work.

A careful examination of the picture indicates that Renoir has been accurate in his drawing and layout. What he has done is to subordinate finish to a brilliance of surface. It is of interest to note that, though the result bears little resemblance, Renoir's palette here is close to that of his favorite, Veronese.

See color plate V

35

36 Fruits from the Midi, 1881

20 × 25⅝ inches

The Art Institute of Chicago. Mr and Mrs Martin A. Ryerson Collection

This canvas, which is two years earlier than Mme Clapisson (No. 45), is done in precisely the same technique, except that here the painter has used a white canvas and left the ground untoned. The structure of the picture is of the simplest: a blue-and-white plate set well back upon a table covered with a white cloth. The point of view is, as usual, set high with the emphasis entirely upon the rendering of the forms. The palette is unusually bright, with a use of much more vermilion, carmine, and truly bright yellow in contrast, with the last, to the painter's beloved Naples yellow. The fruits are peppers, lemons, tangerines, tomatoes, egg-plants, and pomegranates. The technique used is one of medium-long brushstrokes alternated upon the diagonal. The background is built up of various shades of blue, rose, yellow, emerald green, and grey to achieve the effect of an especially luminous grey. The table cloth is built of touches of white with interbrushed accents of blue and grey. Similar diagonal hatchings at small scale are used to achieve the forms of the fruits, and it is clear that the artist was reacting to his encounters with early Italian techniques.

The major characteristic of the picture is that it epitomizes Renoir's characteristic technique of his earlier period, insofar as pictorial construction and the use of paint are concerned. What is slightly unusual is the real brilliance and intensity of the colors employed, for like most traditionally great colorists, Renoir built his whole system of color upon a relatively limited palette with relatively little pure color in great quantity. Here the case is different: there are considerable areas of the three primary colors, at points almost saturated, pure, and un-altered. The viewer discovers after some time in observing the picture that, the impasto excepted, the concept of the whole painting, its design included, is like that of a piece of decorated chinaware seen at a greatly magnified scale. (It is also plain that while any subject was possible for Renoir to render, he seems to have preferred flowers to fruit for intimate, inanimate objects.)

36

37   Venice – Fog, 1881

$21\frac{1}{4} \times 25\frac{5}{8}$ inches

Lent by Mr and Mrs David Lloyd Kreeger, Washington, D.C.

This is one of the painter's most thoroughly Impressionist works, far more so, indeed, than most of the contemporaneous works by Monet. Here one can see the painter's preoccupation with the ornamentation of the surface of the picture, actually an entirely solid paint layer, with even a considerable impasto. He achieves the most precisely rendered but vaguely defined areas of closely related colors and values, of blue-greys, pinks, tawny ochres, with accents in blue and Naples yellow. By this means the painter has done two things: One is the simple ornamentation and preservation of the surface on which he was working, no mean accomplishment in itself. The other is to render the effect of fog and rippling, even turbulent, water, with architectural forms so indistinctly portrayed that they seem felt rather than seen. The picture is paradigm of such a representation, as well as being a totally convincing evocation the phenomenon of Venice.

Renoir was always sympathetic to natural effects, and his renderings of Venice show this sympathy in especially appealing and convincing ways, as a glance at No. 35 will also show. Venice was, from the time of Carpaccio and the Bellini, a favorite subject for representation, down, at least, till the end of the nineteenth cenutry. Yet its very picturesqueness, as well as the atmospheric effects which surround it from the lagoon make it a deceptively simple subject. (It is a nice point to determine how accurate Guardi and Canaletto really were in their *reportage*.) This picture is, incidentally, one of Renoir's relatively few essays in simple reporting, with only the barest minimum of representation altered to suit his purposes of design or ornamentation. What is present is a strict concern with the effect of light as seen in sky and water, a careful recreation of optical effects. In this he long anticipates the Monet of the *Nymphéas*, for the latter was always seeking the recreation of optical truth (a fact plainly evident in the works which he himself actually completed.)

This concern with light in space was to occupy Renoir but briefly. His concern was to be with the building of pictorial structures which successfully combine form, light, and structure, and simultaneously preserve the sense of a flat surface on which they are achieved.

37

38   Ali, the Young Arab, 1882   (D406)

$20\frac{1}{8} \times 10\frac{3}{4}$ inches

Lent by Mr and Mrs Sidney F. Brody, Los Angeles

This picture, one result of a trip to Algeria, is a direct and utterly sympathetic recording of what was, for the painter, a fascinating alien type. The youth is seen and rendered in the simplest way, with delicate and gentle brushstrokes. He is drawn with finesse, and the spatial representation, though elementary, records the bright wall and shadow of the Casbah, and its rocky, clay street.

Visually, the painting is an extraordinary tour-de-force of design. The pattern in two dimensions is perfectly simple: a large C-form eats into the wall and envelops the form of the boy. He seems to emerge and, at the same time, obstinately remain a part of the two-dimensional pattern. Pattern and spatial structure are so rudimentary, that it is hard for the viewer to realize the brilliance of the simple solution.

The simplicity of the pictorial structure is further obscured by the fact that the character of the observation is precise, even in its very casualness. The painting illustrates neatly the fact that "importance" in a work of art not only has little to do with actual size, it also has even less to do with "importance" of subject matter or grandiosity of expression.

Incidentally, in the ninety years since it was painted, the painting has had but four owners. The first owner, who bought it soon after it was painted, was Mme Clapisson's husband. (The painting fetched 2,850 gold francs at his sale twelve years later.) It then went to the great collector, Viau; in 1937 to Coutot; and, finally, to its present owners.

38

39 Chrysanthemums, 1882

21½ × 26 inches

The Art Institute of Chicago. Mr and Mrs Martin A. Ryerson Collection

This picture is painted at the greatest speed upon a fine linen canvas primed for the occasion. What the viewer sees is a brown earthenware crock (made for kitchen use) set upon what probably is an octagonal-topped guéridon which has been covered with a decorated cloth; it is not clear whether the decorations were embroidered or printed upon the surface. The flowers are life-sized, and consist of white chrysanthemums of a mauve cast, and yellow ones of a golden brown cast. The background is in tones of russet, which are achieved with touches of cobalt blue, burnt and raw umber, and crimson lake. The table cloth is rendered in touches of blue, green, and malachite, with bits of yellow. The pottery jug, which in reality was of dull salt-glazed raw umber earthenware, is rendered in touches of green, blue, and yellow, just as the flowers themselves are enlivened by touches of complementary hues to enrich the substance of the picture as a whole. Save for the dabs of Naples yellow and white lead there is almost no impasto. The entire painting is achieved with essentially transparent washes applied in small patches, much as Cézanne was applying his paint, but with a different aim, because, for one thing, Renoir is not using areas of color as a part of his method of drawing but, rather, as an adjunct to his drawing, and as a means of rendering the reality he saw and wished his beholder to see.

It is difficult to imagine or remember a more persuasive example of Renoir at his most direct and simplest. Indeed, the means are so meager that the viewer is all but unaware of them and, for example, accepts the high eye level as part of his own experience, even as he would have if he were to glance down at the covered guéridon in Renoir's studio. It also demonstrates the ease with which Renoir had devised his own adaptation of the medium of painting in oil (based as it was upon his knowledge of china decoration and window-shade painting), for never does the presence of a white lead painting surface count for more than it does here, and never does the viewer feel more as though to be looking over the painter's shoulder as he worked.

39

40 Charles and Georges Durand-Ruel, 1882 (D410)

$25\frac{1}{2} \times 32$ inches

Lent by Durand-Ruel, Paris

Renoir's dealer's two sons are seen half-length on the bench in a garden. Charles is seated at the left, slightly turned, with his arm stretched out on the top of the bench behind his brother, who is slouched comfortably, directly faced towards the spectator, his arms folded, with a cigar in his left hand. His suit is dull blue, and both young men wear white ties. Each suit is worked with a considerable addition of pinks and yellows to achieve a pale fawn color for the elder brother; a rich, medium dark blue for the younger. The screen of foliage and flowers behind them is done in a tapestry-like juxtaposition of various closely related greens and blues with pink accents. The brush touches are rich and thick with a great amount of variation in their application.

The painting marks what is perhaps the end of the artist's first mature manner, but already in the heads one sees the beginning traces of his dry style. There are distinct lines visible, and there is a feeling of the sense of airlessness which was to mark the dry manner, brilliant light, but no softening through the appearance of an atmospheric haze. The impressive aspect of this painting, aside from the obvious character and stylishness of the portraits as such, is the remarkable pattern in three dimensions. The rectangle really is broken into three large areas, two smaller ones, and two tiny ones. These are themselves organized into definite areas of color varied and ornamented by variations in dark and light and by the changes of texture which describe both the patterns of leaves and flowers and also of shimmering light patterns upon surfaces.

Renoir was not involved with searching as much as with evolving. This aspect is clearly brought out in this picture.

Charles and Georges Durand-Ruel. Photographs taken about 1886

40

41 The Daughters of Durand-Ruel, 1882 (D411)

$32 \times 25\frac{3}{4}$ inches

Lent by the Chrysler Museum at Norfolk, Virginia. Gift of Walter P. Chrysler, Jr

Renoir did not much care for commissioned portraits, and was at his best when he painted his friends and their families. This great picture is no exception, and, indeed, it is so successful that it is always a surprise to discover that, far from being life-sized as one rather expects, the painting is, in fact, rather a small one, just over two-and-a-half feet high. The methods the painter has used are familiar enough, with the horizon set a quarter of the way down from the top of the painting. The English-style garden bench, here in green-blue paint rather than natural weathered teak, is set slightly at an angle to the surface of the picture. The right end of the picture extends beyond the surface of the picture. The first thing visible at the right is a patch of still-life upon the seat, then the younger sister, Jeanne, perched in a slightly uncomfortable position next to her elder sister, Marie-Thérèse. The latter holds a bouquet in her lap and wears a Milan straw hat with a huge red bow and red-lined brim. Various shrubs are visible behind the young women, and a great pocket of space opens directly above their heads and is formed by the V of the tops of the shrubbery.

The most dazzling thing about this canvas is the mastery with which Renoir has managed his paint surface, his colors, the effect of light and air, and, most important of all, the effect of filtered, dappled sunlight upon his subjects.

This portrait must rank as one of the painter's most impressive, if only because it so neatly embodies that art which hides itself and the skill which makes the end possible. Renoir's ostensible and literal subject is the portrayal of the daughters of an intimate friend, which portrayal is done in a masterly way. He does more than that, for he established his sitters not only into a particular place, but also, in the doing, suggests a particular time, with the result that a whole ambiance is created out of the raw materials of the observation of the effects of sunlight upon two pretty young women seen in a garden on a summer day. The entire canvas is a carefully organized pattern of brushwork and color to achieve this end. The whites of the costumes actually function to reflect the surrounding colors and, more important, to emphasize them. The greens, yellows, browns, and reds are more intense because of the whites of the dresses, with their faded quotations of the same colors.

See color plate VI

41

42 The Green Jardinière, 1882 (D412)

$36\frac{1}{2} \times 27$ inches

Lent by The Toledo Museum of Art, Toledo, Ohio. Gift of Edward Drummond Libbey

In this canvas one sees familiar accessories of the Renoir household, the piano, music, and books, and the shiny bronze jardinière, combined with the rendering of a girl, seated and at her ease. Her costume seems to be a shift, somewhat *déshabillée*, with the left sleeve dropped well below the shoulder, and the dull green sash serves both as a spatial accent and as a repetition of the color of the plant container. The touches of paint are free and loose with a moderate impasto contrasted with relatively thin passages as well as a few bits of the visible canvas.

The emphasis in the picture is upon a contrast between the sitter seen in a relatively soft focus contrasted against the sharpness and clarity of the metallic surface of the jardinière and the sconce of the piano, which latter item serves to accentuate the reality of the spatial void between the foreground and the upright front of the piano. The background, in the relative far distance, is softly focused and blends into and even confuses itself with the forms of the leaves in the middle distance.

It is only after a precise examination of the painting that it becomes apparent that the artist has taken some liberties with the actual reality he was rendering. The woman who occupies the nominal front block of space is heroic in scale in comparison with that of the piano, while the plant in its container is heroic in contrast with the woman. What, thus, appears as a straightforward, naturalistic picture, is, in fact, an arbitrarily distorted statement of reality. This fact is even more striking if one examines the drawing of the woman herself, for the structure of her anatomy as it is rendered is curious in the extreme with her neck wildly off center and her head in an impossible position. The head, moreover, is actually out of scale with the rest of the body. But Renoir has adjusted his shapes and his forms as they exist in space to suit his own purpose: to achieve a carefully designed and rendered reality which is more convincing than a mere version could ever be.

42

43   City Dance, 1883   (D440)

101 × 34¾ inches

Lent by Durand-Ruel, Paris

This painting is perhaps the most solidly achieved painting Renoir ever did of the female form. The figure of the woman (Suzanne Valadon, the mother of Utrillo) is precisely, even lovingly, drawn, and the emphasis upon the flesh on her arms and back, as well as the structure of her chin and head, is matched by the skill with which the surface of her hair, and the textures not only of her skin but of her gloves and dress are achieved. The same is true of figure of the largely hidden man who is her partner (Paul Lhote, a friend of Renoir's in the shipping trade), and it is only after the viewer sees the pattern of the man's bangs and the tails of his coat does it become apparent that the artist has concentrated upon a sense of motion, something unusual for him.

The sense of decoration, of the ornamenting of a painted surface, with figures isolated before the pervasive shape and area of the floor, the column and its wall, and the palms and flowers in the conservatory, is paramount in the painting. While in no sense does the painting resemble Veronese, one is, indeed, reminded of some of the Venetian's decorative accomplishments. This effect is heightened by the contrast between the dark blue – almost black – of the man's suit and the dazzling white of the woman's attire.

The colors are set out upon a toned ground, and they are juxtaposed with the greatest care for establishing not only the reality of local color but also to maintain the sense of light and air and, simultaneously, retain the sense of the flat surface of the canvas. It well may have been the desire to maintain the sense of a flat surface ornamented by touches of almost pure color which accounts for Renoir's quite consistent use of a high horizon with its effect of the scene viewed from a height, a method familiar in Japanese prints but hardly a source for the painter. The painting as it has finally evolved is basically a rectangle divided into a blue-green quarter, a rose-gold quarter, a greyed-ivory quarter, with the remaining quarter the displaced white of the dress, which is interlocked into the dark of the suit, a pattern as contrived and subtle as that of a work by Braque.

See color plate VII

43

44 Country Dance, 1883 (D441)

$101 \times 34\frac{3}{4}$ inches

Lent by Durand-Ruel, Paris

The space of the painting is carefully divided in two dimensions to achieve a pair of contrasted patterns. The first is that of the top third of the canvas in opposition to that of the bottom third: a textured dark (the foliage, and blues and greens) against a plain bottom third: a light floor. The plain dark of the man's suit (the jacket and trousers subtly contrasted in color and tone) is set against the woman's dress which is intensely light, with a texture derived from the tiny pattern of the fabric. (The man is again Paul Lhote, and the woman is Aline Charigot, who became Renoir's wife.) The woman's fan in the upper left of the canvas contrasts with the man's hat set on the floor in the lower right of the picture. The three-dimensional structure of the work is carefully rendered, but it contains some surprises. The space, as it is indicated by the gallery rail, recedes in a fashion not consonant with the scale of the principal figures. This inconsistency makes the figures even more heroic than the artist has drawn them. The receding perspective of the rumpled table and the rush-bottomed chair is highly distorted, and the orthogonal formed by the balcony rail at the left could not have quite existed in terms of that of the edge of the table at the right. The resultant distortion of spatial reality is not especially noticeable, nor, moreover, is the ambiguous spatial situation of the dancing couple on the ground below the balcony. This latter couple not only serves as a focal closing point in the spatial structure but also as a counter-balance to the cup with the spoon in it upon the table.

The clarity of the forms of the two great dancing figures is equalled only by the skill with which they are drawn and by the beauty of the paint touches. The solidity and lucidity of the man's left hand clutching the woman's right wrist are equalled by the care with which her fingers touch the blades of her fan. Further, the softness and scope of the colors, all soft in hue and tone, set upon the toned ground but transparent enough to permit the white of the ground to function, are of the greatest richness in chromatic effect.

44

45 Madame Clapisson, 1883 (D433)

$31\frac{1}{4} \times 25\frac{1}{4}$ inches

The Art Institute of Chicago. Mr and Mrs Martin A. Ryerson Collection

Léon-Marie Clapisson was a well-to-do collector who commissioned Renoir to paint his wife. His first portrait of her (D428, see below), shows Mme Clapisson seated among the brilliant roses of her garden, full length, and both the sitter and her husband hated it and refused it (see below). This picture is Renoir's second try and remains a perfect fashionable portrait or more accurately, the perfect likeness of a fashionable woman of great and understated *chic*. She is seated on the diagonal towards the picture plane with her head turned directly toward the viewer. (The chair of tufted rose silk appears in other works by the painter.) She wears an ornament of white plumes in her closely coiffed hair, earrings, gloves (to judge from their shimmer) of champagne colored *glacé* kidskin, some discreet but elegant bracelets, and she holds her white plumed fan with white silk ribbons in her folded, relaxed hands. Her dark cobalt blue dress appears to be made of soft, shimmering satin which is covered with chiffon of the same color. Nothing could be simpler or more elegant in its concentration on the sitter's lovely arms, chest, neck, and bosom of which she (and her husband) were obviously proud, so it is no wonder they rejected a representation of her *en tailleur* lost at a distance among the flowers.

The painting is brilliant both for concept and execution. On the white lead ground a second ground has been applied, over which Renoir laid a toner of intense raw sienna with almost a russet glow. Directly onto this prepared surface, Renoir has set his subject in the most direct kind of painting with the subtlest variation in the hues of the skin: pale pink, palest Naples yellow, cool greenish white, and shadows of a soft green amber cast. The blue of the dress is reflected under her right arm. Around the figure Renoir set in his background of muted blue, mauve, grey, dull, dark yellow and bits of russet; but he lets the ground function as a line around her shoulder and her right arm.

Renoir has evoked the effect of gaslight upon flesh and the effect of a face covered in enamel. It is hardly probable that he painted by gaslight; but here he has evoked the character of its special kind of illumination most convincingly.

The picture is a miracle of compression, simplicity, and elegance apposite to the subject. In this picture one can view Renoir's consummate professionalism at work, and while he did not really like commissioned portraits, especially of demanding sitters, he here devoted himself to delivering what the client wanted. One also sees how Renoir put his picture together and how magnificently he did it. The painting is the absolute summation of his technical mastery and distinction.

See color plate VIII

D428 Private Collection, New York

45

46 Lucie Berard, Child in White, 1883 (D449)

24¼ × 19¾ inches

The Art Institute of Chicago. Mr and Mrs Martin A. Ryerson Collection

This is a directly painted portrait of a child in an elegant tucked linen shirt, on which she wears an overdress of ivory white stuff like a flannel with an embroidered yoke and ivory buttons. (Lucie was the daughter of a rich banker and former embassy secretary, Paul Bérard, who was one of the artist's major patrons.) The child stands at attention, standing in her best clothes so that the painter could work from her.

The canvas has scumbles of yellows and siennas over the white lead priming. On to this Renoir has painted the background which is thin and very freely and unevenly scumbled. The child, on the contrary, is painted with a solid paint film, and in the costume areas a considerable amount of delicate impasto. Renoir has drawn Lucie's hands with great care and clearly shows her smooth and soft flesh. Her head is rendered to appear most solid with, again, the smooth skin lovely painted, as is also her brilliant golden hair. She obviously had big blue eyes, and the painter very reasonably has made these the focal point of the picture. Surprisingly enough, Lucie is shown with her glance directed not at the spectator but slightly away from him.

As a work of art the painting not only evokes childhood in general, as well as a particular little girl, but it also is a brilliant piece of abstract design in the simplest of terms. There is no sense of space, only of light and color. And the sole indication of air is in the fact that Lucie's hands are in slightly softened focus. The total impression is slightly uncompromising and a bit austere. This is perhaps the result of Renoir's own attitudes towards the progress of his work.

The attached photograph shows Lucie at a slightly later age.

Photograph of Lucie Bérard *Courtesy M. Daulte*

46

47   The Afternoon of the Children at Wargemont, 1884   (D457)

50 × 68¼ inches

Lent by Nationalgalerie, Staatliche Museen, Preussischer Kulturbesitz, Berlin

After Renoir's Impressionist crisis, he achieves (with the Tyson *The Bathers*, in Philadelphia) his greatest synthesis in his dry manner in this noble work. The spell of the Renaissance, and its simple forms, has worked on the painter. The observation of surfaces and forms is as sharp as ever, but there is a simplification and smoothing of the surfaces to achieve the feeling of solidity. And Renoir has defined his space far more accurately and fully than usual and he has lowered his horizon line within the room. (The garden outside is either a hillside, or conceived on a different system of orthogonals.)

The three daughters of Paul Bérard are found in a Louis XVI room paneled in pale blue. There appear to be curtains of embroidered Indian stuff (they may be of chintz), a Louis XVI table or dressing table covered with a Turkoman or Caucasian rug, and a bowl of nasturtiums in the window sill. The oldest girl, Marthe, is seated on a Louis-Philippe ballroom chair while her youngest sister, Lucie, in front of her, places a doll on her lap; a second older sister, Marguerite, is absorbed in her book, seated on a Louis XVI canapé. The use of color is extraordinary with the cool hues on one side, the warm ones on the other. But the warm ones are cool, with the vermilion stockings of Marthe cast in a cool light. The harmony is based on cobalt blue, Naples yellow, and vermilion, all heightened with white and deepened with ochre and raw umber. The patterns and shapes are as precisely rendered as the effect of light on the surface.

Yet the picture is not a return to Raphael or Ingres. It merely shows how much the painter had learned from them when he mellowed and solidified his style. For clarity of form and articulation into the spatial structure, this is Renoir's greatest solution, and it is one of his greatest pictures.

See color plate IX

47

48   Paul Haviland, 1884   (D454)

$22\frac{5}{8} \times 17$ inches

Lent by Nelson Gallery – Atkins Museum (Nelson Fund), Kansas City, Missouri

Four-year-old Paul Haviland (the son of the Limoges china manufacturer), is dressed in a sailor suit and leans his arms at rest on top of a plain Louis XVI table with complete poise. This is one of the painter's most directly observed and rendered portraits. As an image of childhood it is especially captivating. The little boy's suit is of richly varied cobalt blue, and beneath his jacket with the wide white-bordered revers, is a standard sailor's horizontally striped jersey pullover of which the sleeves and neckline are discreetly ruffled. The child's face is rendered with bright pink cheeks, clearly radiant skin, and the almond eyes which had become one of Renoir's hallmarks. Young Paul's hair is medium blonde and closely cropped. Perhaps the most wonderful part of the rendering is his hands which are exquisitely drawn and as suavely modeled in delicate warm and cool touches of color.

The dark background is somewhat unusual, and just as unexpected is the absence of any specifically rendered place. The color is a rich amalgam of warm browns with crimson accents. As sometimes happens, Renoir has reverted to a scheme he had used long before. Here he is recalling the portrait of his father (No. 7) of fifteen years before. The difference is the simple one of having so manipulated his paint that the boy's face seems slightly in softened focus. Actually, an examination will show that the face is clearly, even sharply rendered. What appears soft is the child's skin. Renoir has developed the sense of a flickering light upon his subject which is barely implicit in his father's portrait. Here the light fairly shimmers. It is this quality of varied light that gives the picture a lively quality, enhances the presence of the sitter, and even suggests his imminent lively movements, which were temporarily stilled for the picture. This is so successfully done that one realizes the way the painter had with all children, that he could get so obviously a lively youngster to remain calm and not sulk.

48

49 Portrait of a Young Girl, 1884 (D460)

22½ × 18 inches

Lent by Edwin C. Vogel, New York

This portrait is Renoir's considered evocation of Renaissance form (and even technique) in its attempt to reconstruct in the rather dry manner of Italian fresco painting something of the austerity which he seems to have felt missing from his work. On first glance the picture seems straightforward enough, and it is only on reflection that one realizes that elegant young Parisian women did not indeed often go about wearing their hair full and flowing beneath an elegant sun-shading straw hat and in proper street dress and rather grand gold earrings.

What Renoir has done is to render meticulously in the most delicate, hatched technique the physical presence and fullness of the beauty of a very real French woman. But he has done this through the discipline of delicate hatching strokes which are the disciplined opposite – or so he seems to have felt – of the loose and flowing touches one notes in the *Chrysanthemums* of three years earlier (No. 39). It is rather as though Renoir had thought of one of Titian's half-length females or Veronese's in this evocation of female beauty. One may suspect that he began his painting with a clear idea of how he wanted to achieve it, but that the resemblance and remembrance of the great Venetians did not occur to him till he was well along in his painting of this picture. The only really Venetian characteristics lie in the gesture of the hair held in the hand, the pendant earring, and the nobility of the forms. What is emphatically not Venetian is the technique of applying the paint, for Veronese in his frescoes never seems to be thinking back to the late Gothic and here one feels that Renoir was at least remembering what Cennino had said about putting on paint.

For all of the memories of Venice which Renoir evokes, his use of color and the patches of color in the background are particularly his own. Especially so is the device of placing his subject into a state of chromatic nowhere so that she emerges from a haze of color.

49

50 The River God, 1885 (D475)

$21\frac{5}{8} \times 57\frac{1}{8}$ inches

Lent by Dr Walter Feilchenfeldt, Zürich

Renoir has in this middle period, highly decorative work, taken the familiar late antique motif of the river-god, especially as it is known both from Roman artifacts, but also from the figures from the Medici tombs, as well as from Sansovino fountain figures. The grandly scaled figure in the foreground not only quotes the prototypes but is, in fact, quite closely observed from the model, whereas the landscape fragment and the waterfall in the left-hand far distance seem very much a product of the painter's imagination.

The painter's method anticipates the great late decorative works, and in this instance the picture reflects precisely in its technique Renoir's reaction to Italian fresco methods. The very nature of the fresco, with its hatching technique done in watercolor, obviously struck a resonant chord in Renoir's mind. After all, the method is essentially that which he knew so well from the decoration of chinaware. It is the discipline of the method, curiously enough, which enabled Renoir to pursue both the extension of his pictorial method – which in his case was to make his variety of Impressionism as solid and monumental as Cézanne sought for himself – and to reassert the fundamentally conservative aspect of his artistic nature. Renoir was traditionalist at heart, but his traditionalism was not of a sort which had degenerated into a fossilized dogmatism. Rather, in such a work as this, Renoir recognized both the majesty of Michelangelo and Annibale, and also the solid accomplishments of both Poussin and the giants of eighteenth-century painting in France. Renoir's pursuit of color in this picture is as carefully considered as Cézanne's was, and in its own way it is as artificial and disciplined.

Perhaps the most impressive technical aspect of this painting lies in its extraordinary anticipation of Renoir's last manner, for in his restricted and limited color, in the heroic cast of the forms, the softness of focus, and the insistence on both the solidity of his shapes and the concomitant flatness of the picture plane, one already is almost looking at *Alexander Thurneyssen as a Shepherd* (No. 80).

50

51   Madame Renoir, 1885   (D484)

$25\frac{5}{8} \times 21\frac{1}{4}$ inches

Lent by the Philadelphia Museum of Art. W. P. Wilstach Collection

This direct and gentle representation is entirely plausible as a first-rate likeness of Aline, but one notes that the painter has limited his vision under austere self-discipline to achieve a monumental image. The discipline purified and simplified Renoir's expression in pursuing optical and pictorial truths, and the artist was here far more interested in the pictorial whole than in rendering mere optical truths for their own sake.

Renoir has here abandoned the illusionism which occupied him in his portrait of Paul Haviland of the year before (No. 48). This dry style was Renoir's painful search for something as solid as Cézanne sought. This new pursuit sent him to a sharpened focus in representation, the result of both seeing the old Italian masters and also looking once more at Boucher. Once he had satisfied himself through the painful method he was trying, he then could return to the problems of pictorial organization with the awareness that he might safely, in Dr. Johnson's phrase, abandon his mind to them.

But there is no frenzy in this painting, only disciplined order with a resultant serenity. A fascinating sidelight to this picture is that in his own simplification he has anticipated some of the austerities of the young Picasso of a generation after this.

51

Madame Renoir with Pierre, 1886 (D496)

31½ × 25½ inches

Lent by the Norton Simon Foundation, Los Angeles

Aline is seen here nursing the oldest Renoir son, Pierre, in June, 1886. This is the second of three versions of this scene, the first in Paris, and the last in an American private collection. Renoir's color usage here is not unlike Cézanne's, with the patches of color built up with contrasting hues to set them off and enrich them, something especially noticeable in the skirt where the grey and cobalt are enlivened with touches of red and yellow ochres. The impact of Italian fresco technique is clearly visible here, and the tonality is basically that of a fourteenth-century wall painting – pale, in muted colors, with an especially delicate understanding of Naples yellow.

The forms have been simplified and in some cases altered (the neck is enlarged), and Renoir has presented an icon rather than a mere reproduction of what he saw. Yet the viewer is jerked sharply back to reality by the veristic handling of the rattan chair, the texture of the stone parapet, and the arabesque made by the yellow leaves of the tree above the figures. As a new father Renoir found the subject appealing, but he renders it not only without sentimentality but even without comment. Rather, he gives a fundamental aspect of maternity in terms which go back to antiquity.

The technique is in the painter's driest manner with the paint touches done as hatching strokes and no blending of the paint. He might just as easily have made the same picture in a variety of egg tempera as far as the use of the paint is concerned.

52

53 Standing Nude, 1887 (D521)

32 × 20 inches

Lent by a Private Collector

Renoir has here concentrated his interest on the beauty of the female figure in its textures, forms, and colors. He has set these off by the contrast with the draped garment and the brilliantly suggested surround of landscape. This latter is a kind of Neverland accomplished in its coloration and touches to suggest a few leaves and flowers. The background emphasizes the nature and qualities of the figure and serves as a shimmering area from which it has emerged.

Renoir, passionately absorbed in the antique, has quoted the Venus of Melos. But one may be reasonably sure that if the quotation occurred to him consciously, it did so only when the painting was well on its way to completion. Antiquity is evoked even more strongly in the resolution of the anatomy and its simplification than rather in the pose, and though the coiffure is Praxitelean, the model's head is obstinately French from the early years of the Third Republic. This is part of the artist's magic, for with all of his evocations of the past, he always stayed straightforwardly French and of his own time.

If Mme DuBarry loved Sèvres plaques on her furniture, so also did the rich bourgeois love elegant wall ornaments in the guise of paintings such as this one. This is but one more example of the straightforwardness of mind which the painter's years as a china and shade decorator had left with him and which firmly supported his native temper to avoid the self-indulgent.

53

54   Antibes, 1888

$25\frac{1}{2} \times 32$ inches

Lent by The Armand Hammer Foundation, Los Angeles

In a curious fashion Renoir has here combined motifs which are straight out of both Corot and Claude, done, of course, directly from nature. The intensity of the light is rendered in strictly Impressionist terms and through the methods of the Impressionists: the sky is rendered in touches of yellows, pinks, and whites as well as a variety of blues, which all combine to suggest the intensity of the brilliant light of the Mediterranean world on a summer day. The intensity of the light as well as the haze in the atmosphere are rendered so as to push the mountains in the far distance back almost out of sight. In this accomplishment the painter fills his canvas with a sense not only of light but also of atmosphere.

Rather atypically, Renoir has here employed a relatively low horizon. This has the slightly disconcerting effect of making the patch of landscape function even as more of a *répoussoir* than it normally would, and the emphasis is upon the absolute solidity of the structure of the earth, with the rocks beneath tacitly acknowledged. The depth and distance of the landscape is neatly described by the garden wall, which is seen to recede into the distance, with the figures of the people rendered almost as painted monuments in the landscape rather than as mere *staffage*.

Perhaps the most surprising thing about the picture is the richness, intensity, and variety of the colors used in rendering the landscape itself. Here the painter actually departs from natural appearances, for the colors he has shown are those normally visible in such intensity only on an overcast or rainy day. What he has done is to combine the visible of a rainy landscape with that of a sunny sky and sea. The result is slightly disconcerting as it suggests a dislocation of the sense of time as it affects the viewer's sense of place. In this concept Renoir has rendered an ideal world which, in its terms, is as artificial as those of Poussin or Claude. Yet Renoir's adjustment and intensification of reality is so artfully done that it is only upon careful reflection that the viewer realizes the impossibility of the picture as he sees it. Rather, he accepts Renoir's transformation of natural phenomena.

54

55 Two Girls at the Piano, 1889 (D561)

$22 \times 18\frac{1}{4}$ inches

Lent by Joslyn Art Museum, Omaha

This version of the motif of women at the piano is cast in the relatively sharply focused manner of the artist towards 1890. There is a softening of contours but still a precise emphasis on solidity of modelling and realization of the forms themselves as well as absolute precision in the drawing. The piano which is so hazy in the canvas of fifteen years before (No. 20) is not rendered with absolute descriptive accuracy. (One notes that in the interim Mme Renoir appears to have replaced the piano stool with a new one; this time by or in the manner of Thonet in bent wood and probably with a caned seat.) Instead of the harmony of blue-green and pinkish white with shimmering nacreous tones, the scheme is now one of dark browns, mauves, and a variety of warm reds and Naples yellow and gold. One notes that the room has been redecorated, and that a curtain indeed is at the end of the room and, thus, separates the space from another, one of which is an alcove.

What Renoir has done is to remember the example of the relative clarity of focus throughout the picture which he had observed not only in Italian frescoes but also in the works of Boucher and Fragonard. This picture is in the straightforward genre tradition of eighteenth-century France, and the clarity of presentation is here worthy of Chardin and comparable to his example. In this painting Renoir demonstrates that he has achieved in his terms what Cézanne stated as his goal, to make of the Impressionist method something comparable to the 'art of the museums' – in other words to restate formal solidity after the pursuit of the evanescence of light alone, as had happened in certain earlier works.

As Renoir's brush touches never failed him, the surface of the picture, its *matière*, in the French word, is still ravishing. But in this transitional moment just before the last manner, smoothness and solidity is achieved by the suppression of brushwork for its own sake.

55

56 Washerwomen, 1886–1889 (D572)

22¼ × 18½ inches

Lent by the Baltimore Museum of Art. The Cone Collection

This genre bit is done in a technique which is remarkably close to that of Pissarro but with the inevitable change which occurs in Renoir's concept of female form. In its way the painting is as close to an illustration as can be found in all of Renoir's work, simply because of its casual anecdotal quality. In the foreground is an overturned basket with clothes spilled upon the ground. Behind it, on the diagonal and up on the picture surface are two kneeling women at work scrubbing clothes. Behind them to the right a small child in a smock stands, hands clasped behind, in converation with another woman who is standing and has paused in her work. Behind her is a tree, behind that a house, and beyond that, trees and a field which disappear into the usual high horizon.

Except for the forms of the figures, the technique is one of long, streaked strokes, done in parallel slashes. The faces and arms of the women are worked in much thinner, less obtrusive strokes. The arms of the two kneeling women make a remarkable arabesque, and the contrast between the parts of the women's bodies and the folds of their clothes is carefully and subtly accomplished. The whole of the canvas is broken into small areas of color which are also small areas of form. The space is empirically rendered, and while it is believable enough, in no sense is it achieved with much real sense of structure. Renoir, once his women were painted, apparently concentrated his attention upon describing the landscape in terms which echo and parallel the women's own forms and shapes, so that there is a considerable amount of visual metaphor.

The final impression engendered by the picture is that it is one on which the painter devoted especial care but that it is not one in which the resolution of the pictorial problems is especially easy or in any way lyrical in its handling and accomplishment. Yet neither is the work in an austere or hard vein.

56

57 The Apple Seller, 1890 (D585)

$25\frac{7}{8} \times 21\frac{5}{16}$ inches

Lent by The Cleveland Museum of Art. Leonard C. Hanna Jr Collection

This relatively small canvas (a tiny bit over two feet high) is a study not only in the effects of light and shade upon color intensities but also a demonstration of the function of brushwork to describe not only form but to establish spatial concepts. The painting is based upon a harmony of blues and greens (cobalt and emerald in combination) as they are altered by the use of Naples yellow, raw umber, and touches of crimson with a few patches of burnt umber or Van Dyck brown. The presence of the white ground is fundamental to Renoir's purpose in focusing the attention upon the reality of light not only as represented but as a determining factor in the construction of the painting.

The dappled pattern of light and dark, as well as that of alternated colors, establishes a strong sense of the ornamentation of the surface. The seated figures repeat their patterns of design, and the blue contrasts against the warm rose-orange of the middle figure. Both children are set off in color by the white of the mother's gown. The scale of the apples provides a focus for the attention of the spectator, while the little leaping dog provides not only an accent which implies motion in an otherwise still scene, but its color (black, brown, and gold ochre) establishes a punctuation which stops the gaze and closes the structure of the painting. (This small bit of observed action is just that, but it is also a quotation from sixteenth-century Venice.)

The style of the painting epitomizes Renoir's developed late maturity which evolved before that of his last years. Here there is still an emphasis not only upon space but deep space at that. But the patterns of the forms of both the figures and foliage point their way to that of the last years when the picture becomes essentially an ornamented plane which reproduces the effects of a colored high relief.

57

58   Head of a Young Girl, 1890 (D613)

$16\frac{1}{4} \times 12\frac{3}{4}$ inches

The Art Institute of Chicago. Gift of Joseph Winterbotham

Here Renoir has fragmented reality, and the girl with golden hair is lightly brushed into a background of dull green. There is a tawny, dull orange curtain to the viewer's left, and the immediate impression is one of clarity, even ordinariness. The painter has emphasized the texture and color of the sitter's hair through discreet color differentiation, with the Naples yellow strokes predominating.

It is only after careful scrutiny that one notes how much Renoir has adjusted anatomical fact to suit his purpose. The basic anatomical structure is odd and the location of the girl's left breast is odd indeed in relation to the rest of her physique. Of course, by this date the painter recognized the limits of ordinary appearances as they were useful to his visual concepts. It is because Renoir actually was a consummate draughtsman with a breathtaking knowledge of natural form that he was able to take his forms, alter them, adjust them, and reassemble them to achieve a pictorial synthesis infinitely more telling and powerful than any ordinary copying could ever be.

This picture is not only Renoir's tribute to Boucher but also to eighteenth-century Venice and Rome.

58

59 After the Bath, 1890 (D617)

$25\frac{1}{8} \times 21\frac{1}{4}$ inches

Lent by Mr and Mrs Joseph S. Wohl, New York

Renoir's brushwork had become broader with rubbed-in patches once more, and broad washes of paint. The picture is completely monumental in concept, though of rather small format, for the artist had become a complete master of scale and the sense of the grand form. Any particularized sense of space has been abandoned for an imaginery out-of-doors which is accomplished in vague forms to suggest overhanging rocks, a pond, and trees in the distance.

Here he has summarized and simplified the rendering of the surface of the model's skin. The summary is radiant in its emphasis on the effect of light on the skin with a concomitant luminosity and radiance. The forms have also been summarized to make them ampler, bulkier, and more solid than they probably were in reality. This effect is reinforced by the beige tonality.

Part of the monumental effect of this painting is achieved by the omission of any specific locale, but more of it is because the figure dominates the painting by covering most of it. Additionally, the figure occupies most of the three-dimensional reality which is in any fashion specified. In the realest possible way Renoir has presented a figure out of Clodion in heroic and chromatic terms. That his evocation of Clodion's imagery also reminds the viewer of Carrier-Belleuse as well as Rodin merely affirms how very much a part of his own epoch Renoir was. No matter how thoroughly he evoked past masters or his contemporaries, he obstinately remained himself and of his own time. That he changed throughout his time is evidence of his continuing growth and evolution both stylistically and artistically.

59

60   Young Girls Reading, 1890   (D639)

22 × 18¼ inches

Lent by Portland Art Museum, Portland, Oregon

The structure of this painting is achieved through the use of tiny brushstrokes (rather like extensions of Seurat's dots), based on touches of varied pinks, intense yellows (mostly achieved through the use of Naples yellow with but a slight admixture of a brighter color), blues, and emerald green. The harmony of the ochre curtain, shot with mauve, green, and gold touches, contrasts with that of the wall which is rendered in slight, streaky touches of blue, yellow, and green. The picture seems to have a pale, tawny ochre wash over the lead white priming (although this may be only evidence of a discolored natural resin varnish over the surface of the whole canvas). The primary tonality is one of greenish-gold which is enlivened by the light on the figures which is silvery ivory in tonality (also rather obscured by varnish) of breath-taking coolness.

The young sitters are presented in close juxtaposition with fascinating ambiguities in the spatial rendering. The repetition of the figures, indeed, their relative coalescence, contrasts markedly with the rendering of the separation of the two-part back of the *confidante* on which they are sitting. Renoir forces the viewer to look up at his sitters and almost ignores their precise location in space in the room. It is only after a considerable scrutiny of the painting that one becomes aware that the painter has focused the viewer's glance upon the faces of the young women by means of a relative sharpening of the focus in this part of the picture. The repetition of their faces and their hands joined to hold the book, with the space between, forms the heart and visual center of the painting, so that the rest of the picture becomes merely a flat surface ornamented in color.

The whole picture, which might be called a minor work, is one of suavity and serenity. Its accomplishment is such that the viewer must recognize that even a small work by a master always bears the stamp of his way of seeing and always shows a slightly different facet of his talent.

60

61 Young Girls Reading, *c.*1892

32 × 25½ inches

Lent by The Virginia Museum of Fine Arts, Richmond

This picture illustrates the transition from Renoir's styles of the 1880's to that of his last period. After his return to his sort of hard-edged, sharp-focus manner, he then was able again to loosen his manner, yet preserve the solidity and firmness he had sought as the result of years of crisis. The handling here is softened, but the forms themselves are rendered to be clear, simple, and predominant over the very considerable use of ornament not only in the costume but also on the surface of the picture itself. The tonality is rather a subdued one, and this time Renoir has sought a grey and beige tonality with the color accents mainly in rose and gold. The setting is not quite precisely determined, but presumably it is indoors in spite of the fact that the sitters are wearing their very elaborate hats, and that one is seated upon a folding chair. Renoir has been especially precise in his drawing, and the delineation of the hands, arms, the features of the faces, and the forms of the bodies beneath the summer dresses is totally clear and unambiguous.

The palette in this case is clearly derived from that of Italian fresco painting of the Middle Ages and the Renaissance, and the handling of the paint reflects Renoir's reaction to the examples of that intractable medium. Put another way, the handling of the paint, though idiomatic in terms of the oil medium, makes full use of the methods of the frescoist. The palette in this instance is remarkably close to that of Masaccio's Carmine frescoes, and the modelling of the faces in a greenish yellow and raw umber, though long familiar to Renoir, here particularly reveals his awareness of early Italian methods. It is not that Renoir was consciously imitating the past but that, rather, as he got into the creation of a picture, his accumulated memories preconsciously gave him clues and hints as to his methods.

The finish painting in this instance is one of the painter's subtlest and most solid works. Its very understatement and technical perfection prevents its accomplishment from being obvious.

61

62 Place de la Trinité, 1892

$21 \times 25\frac{3}{4}$ inches

Lent by a Private Collector

This view of the garden in front of the Church of the Trinité, Paris, is one of the master's heroic landscapes. It is monumental in scale if fairly small in size, but the concept is as grand, even grandiose, as any Renoir achieved. The composition is begun by half-figures visible at the bottom right of the painting set against the corner of a balustrade. This fragment of an elevation serves as a double *répoussoir* in that the remainder of the landscape is not only pushed back into space but also below into space. It further sets the beholder at a considerably distance in front of the surface of the painting, an effect greatly enhanced by a vanishing point approximately at the middle of the painting a quarter of the way in from the viewer's left. By this accomplishment Renoir convinces the spectator that the scene is part of a much larger whole and continues far beyond the edges of the painting, even though at the same time the scheme of the painting is most carefully considered to an integrated whole.

The front tree on the left side is seen in silhouette with its leaves caught in the sunlight, while the trees beyond it are more completely silhouetted with only a few touches of sunlight. The same is true of the carefully placed flower beds. The middle distance has figures in it which function as *staffage* pieces but in fact are far more than that in their careful observation. The great staircase of the church façade is defined at the right center, with the façade itself seen in terms to echo Veronese. The rear of the scene is closed by blocks of flats seen in receding planes. There is a bright and pervasive sky painted in what is actually a subdued working of blues. The only bright touches in the whole, aside from those of sunlit leaves, are the reds of the flower beds and those in the flags.

The total effect of the painting is that of lush foliage and austerely grand architecture seen in brilliant but dappled light. The sense of life is enhanced by the glowingly glittering figures of the painting which are achieved through tiny brushstrokes in closely contrasted color touches. The result is a synthesis of what went before in Renoir's work.

62

63 Madame Gallimard, 1892

$31\frac{1}{2} \times 25$ inches

Lent from the Collection of Mr and Mrs Robert B. Mayer, Winnetka

Renoir has taken a lively, if not really pretty, woman dressed in the curiously unattractive mode of the 1890's, seated her in an ample rattan chair, and directed her at the audience. Her figure is an ample one, and one senses her form beneath her skirt and notices her exceedingly slender hands clasped at rest on her lap. Her placement in the chair is firmly established, and the chair and its reed are meticulously rendered.

The painting comes to life, because all of this material is subordinated to her face, and she has one of the most compelling presences which Renoir ever painted. Not only is she compelling, even dominating, but the painter has presented her face so as to make it most sympathetic. She has a light smile, and it is successful; occasionally Renoir painted smiling faces, and they often seem merely grotesque. But this subject is sympathetic, and Renoir has even had her open her mouth slightly to reveal handsome teeth and made this device work. Further, her ears are set firmly on to her skull, and their drawing serves to emphasize the reality and solidity of the skull. One's gaze comprehends the simple, even casual coiffure, which, among other things, serves to close the picture design at the top. But the compelling part of the face and, ultimately, the whole painting, are the brilliant, dark eyes set under regular, heavy, dark brows. Renoir has duly recorded the fact that the light on the eye is the light on a sphere, and he has emphasized the glitter and splendor of this part of the woman's appearance. As a face and as a presence, this portrait is one of the painter's most compelling images, even a haunting one.

64   Young Girls and a Little Boy in a Landscape, 1893

25⅝ × 31⅞ inches

Lent by Philip and Janice Levin, New York

This painting shows the painter at work rendering the effect of brilliant light and shade (seen in dappled patches) in terms of relatively broadly brushed patches of paint. The right front triangle of the painting defines the foreground and sets the figures into place. Behind them, also on the diagonal, is a sunlit road, and in the far distance one sees buildings with hills beyond them. The rendering is simple and direct, and the picture seems to be one which caused the painter no problems in conception or execution.

The motif of the three trees with the principal one strongly in the foreground is one worthy of Cézanne, and while Renoir plainly was his own man, it is equally plain that in this instance he has paid homage to his great friend. The whole canvas and its design are cast in the vein of the master of Aix, and this is one of the relatively few canvases in which Renoir so clearly shows his feeling for the methods and vision of his friend.

64

65 Mademoiselle Lerolle Sewing, 1896

$32 \times 25\frac{1}{8}$ inches

Lent from a Swiss Private Collection

One here has a perfect example of Renoir's penultimate style, one in which he has combined absolute clarity of form, simplicity of color, simplifications of textures, with a clear rendering of a light which illuminates but does not overwhelm or coruscate enough to diminish the quality of the forms or obscure the clarity of the drawing. The painter has with the casualness of a photographer caught his subject at work with her embroidery frame neatly accounted for in space and with friends in the next room who are inspecting the pictures on the wall, as usual with the horizon line set very high. As the light represented is very brilliant for an interior light, the contrast of the sunlight upon the men in the background is as intense – if not more so – as it is on the subject of the picture.

In this picture, as in the *Woman in a Boat* (No. 22), there is a firm emphasis upon the solidity of the sitter in the foreground with its contrast of the void of the distance behind her, nearness against farness. This latter quality is emphasized even more strongly by the disparate scale between the figures and by the fact that there is no diminution of the intensity of the background figures through the use of the device of aërial perspective. This is one of Renoir's few pictures in which one is aware of an enveloping sense of light but not of atmosphere.

The painting was achieved by toning the white lead ground with a tawny scumble well rubbed into the surface. Upon this Renoir has painted his picture using watercolor brushes in great part and rather tiny strokes (fresco-like) to achieve his whole. The impasto touches are achieved, presumably, with bristle brushes. Renoir has by the time of this picture synthesized his dry manner with his earlier "wet" style, and in this synthesis he is making possible the breadth of his latest style, a style which, incidentally, was not hampered by his own physical disabilities.

66–67 Two Figures from Oedipus, 1895

$37\frac{1}{2} \times 14$ inches

Lent by Maurice Stuart, Chicago

In the middle 1890's Renoir had been asked by Gallimard, the owner of the Théâtre des Variétés, to do a set of wall decorations from Greek sources for the decoration of a room in his country house. These were to be installed onto Louis XVI panelling. For some reason the project was never finished, and these panels (which Jean Renoir remembers seeing in his parents' Paris flat on the rue Caulaincourt) remained in the studio at the painter's death. There was another pair, almost identical with these but in a more developed state, as well as a number of other sketches for the project. Because they are among the few surviving works which Renoir projected as actual and mural decorations, they are of enormous interest. They are also of great intrinsic interest for they show his most personal reactions to Pompeiian wall paintings. The result is a strange amalgam of the antique style in terms of Renoir's own most idiosyncratic handling. It also reveals most precisely how Renoir's most decorative pictures differ from pure decorations.

Renoir's version of an ancient wall system is done in an 1895 version of Louis XVI with a ghost of the directoire style about it. The figures of *Oedipus* and *Jocasta* (presumably) seem to be quotations from the antique but more probably are the painter's own invention and show him in the process of rendering extremes of emotion in relatively hieratic terms. The female, clad in a diaphanous spotted dress, gesticulates against a flowing red cape, while the male, in yellow with a white toga, points to the ground. At the tops of the panels, bas-reliefs in grisaille are indicated.

Renoir was always absorbed in antiquity, if only from his exposure to ancient sculpture, and, in the last years of his life, in the Mediterranean ambiance. Here he can be seen consciously evoking the past and has also left a precious inkling of how he looked at porcelain painting.

66   67

68 Landscape at Beaulieu, 1897

$25\frac{5}{8} \times 31\frac{7}{8}$ inches

Lent by M. H. de Young Memorial Museum – California Palace of the Legion of Honor, San Francisco

This work of 1897 is done in a surprisingly heavy impasto for its date and with a surprisingly low horizon line. The color scheme is of blue, tan, very dull green, a warmish earth red, a few touches of crimson, and a particularly rich Naples yellow. It is one of the relatively few works in which one can see that occasionally Renoir shared some of Cézanne's attitudes about the laying in of paint and the structure of a landscape. The drawing is precise enough in its rendering, but in an odd way the viewer has a sensation of viewing the scene at some distance with some of the foreground visible to him deliberately omitted in order to emphasize the breadth and fullness of the space portrayed. The garden step makes a firm horizontal accent at the bottom of the picture, while the trees are presented as they exist in space but in diminishingly sharp focus as they recede behind the picture plane. The tree beyond the tropical yucca plants in the foreground rises to the full height of the painting to make a screen through which the sky is visible and beyond which the whole distance is seen in recession.

There is an evenness of accent over the entire surface of the painting which serves to reinforce the sense of the surface of the canvas and also to emphasize the ornamentality of the brushwork itself. Renoir has ornamented his surface even as he had ornamented the surface of Limoges plates so long before.

It is well to remember that the problems which exist for a painter were under such control for Renoir by the time of this work, and the discipline of his craft so great, that the process by which this picture evolved was almost an automatic one. There is no sense of a struggle to communicate nor of problems for resolution. As a perfect master of his craft, Renoir demonstrates in this picture how much the art of painting can be relaxing to a master as the simple working of his *métier*. It is also a painting in which Renoir's intense and truly sensuous pleasure in his work is abundantly clear, if only through the absence of any visible sense of struggle or insecurity of technical control.

68

69   The Artist's Son Jean, 1898

$21\frac{3}{4} \times 18\frac{1}{4}$ inches

The Art Institute of Chicago. Mr and Mrs Martin A. Ryerson Collection

The subject of this captivating painting has described in his essay the circumstances of its creation. What is extraordinary is the sense of light and air which surround the little boy, who, incidentally is rendered at life size, or, if one remembers that he is set a bit behind the picture plane, larger than life. And to this day the picture remains an image of a small child temporarily in repose, seen larger than life, as it were.

That young Jean moved about is evident from the changes his father has made, for there are covered brushstrokes which are now visible which indicated that the hair and the ribbon were altered. The background is thinly painted in the artist's favorite blue, well scrubbed into the surface of the canvas. Into this he has added touches of green and yellow which alter the effect to achieve a sense of shimmering light. The picture was not painted in the studio but in a room in the house, near a window, and one sees the effect of the light which shines in on the child. The red-gold hair is rendered in siennas, umbers, touches of rose, and much Naples yellow. The fabric he holds is done in umber and white, while his smock is worked in red earth with some additions of ochres and crimson. Visually the picture is capped by the bow of pure Naples yellow in his hair, and its effect is so dazzling and so richly cool, that it becomes quite clear why it was one of Renoir's favorite hues, increasingly so to the end of his life.

At some point in its history, before it came to the museum, the painting seems to have been exposed to excessive heat, and the impasto has assumed the wrinkling which is the usual result of such exposure. Apparently in trying to repair the damage, a restorer reworked the surface excessively, so that while the picture seems acceptable on a casual inspection, the use of a binocular microscope reveals a considerable amount of careful but insensitive retouching, much of which seems to be unnecessary.

69

70 Monsieur Germain, 1900

$21\frac{3}{4} \times 18\frac{1}{4}$ inches

Norton Gallery and School of Art, West Palm Beach, Florida

This is a delightful study of a young man who is seen at half length, turned on his chair, his upper right arm visible as it disappears over the chair back, and his left thumb just visible at the edge of the page of a book on a rather high table which is set diagonally towards the plane of the picture. The drawing is notably in soft focus, but one sees clearly the simple jacket and waistcoat, the white shirt with batwing collar and bow tie, and, especially, the double – one might even say, victorious – boutonnière. Finally, one takes in the head with its blond hair, and eyes rendered in soft focus, and the extraordinary moustache. Without this latter feature one sees that the sitter would appear to be a very frail and rather ordinary-looking young man, indeed.

One feels that this picture belongs to the time when the painter had become capable of rendering what he wanted to present in any way he chose and at great speed. One does not know if this portrait was done in one sitting. A glance at the paint surface suggests that it was not, but Renoir has contrived to present an effect which, in fact, suggests that it was. It was part of the real charm of Renoir's work at this period that he could suggest this, for the picture of Mlle Lerolle at her sewing (No. 65) is in the same vein.

One also sees in this picture perhaps part of the explanation of why Renoir increasingly shunned portraiture (except of those he loved) in favor of painting flowers, lanscapes, and nudes. It is not that one feels Renoir was bored when he painted this picture but that, rather, he remained obstinately uninvolved. One may suspect that he preferred painting the boutonnière to painting M. Germain's handsome, rather uninteresting face.

70

71 Villa de la Poste at Cagnes, 1900

$18\frac{1}{4} \times 21\frac{3}{4}$ inches

Lent by Mr and Mrs Josef Rosensaft, New York

This work of 1900 is one of the most solid and austerely realized of Renoir's late landscapes. The palm trees at the left and the flower beds at the right, separated by a garden path, function as *répoussoirs* which direct the viewer's gaze to the sewing woman who is seated on top of a garden wall. Her figure is set off by clumps of foliage, and behind these clumps lie the carefully delineated forms of the houses and wings of them. In the far distance is a mountain range, beyond which is the sky. The horizon is roughly at the center line of the painting.

The color range is limited to the use of dull red tones, a subdued blue, a few touches of bright red, with the whole of the color pattern unified by the pervading and radiant touches of Naples yellow. The use of color is determined by the patterns established by the strokes of the brush which are simple and direct but always placed so as to describe forms and locate their place in the spatial scheme.

Within Renoir's own scheme of things, he has created a painting which is as monumental and solid as a work either by Courbet or Cézanne. It is an achievement which is particularly Renoir's own, and the entire concept is one which states the solidity of the forms which exist in nature, reconstructed in terms not only of the visual experience but also in the particular terms of this painting. In view of the painter's emphasis on the solidity of forms, the intensely felt sense and realization of the pervasiveness of sunlight is rather surprising. It is this carefully achieved fusion of forms seen in light, with concomitant adjustments of scale and forms, which makes the picture seem a huge and almost grandiose work, when, in fact, it is actually rather small. And it is in this canvas that the beholder begins to get an awareness of what the estate of Les Collettes meant to the painter during the last years of his life.

See color plate X

71

72 Reclining Nude, 1902

$26\frac{1}{2} \times 60\frac{5}{8}$ inches

Lent by the Museum of Modern Art, New York. Gift of Mr and Mrs Paul Rosenberg, 1956

The great figure, in a tradition which goes directly back to Giorgione by way of Boucher and Titian, is practially a pendant to the *River God* (No. 50) done seventeen years before. If the husky nymph's genealogy is clear enough, it must not be forgotten that she is Renoir's special creation. He set out to do a monumental nude, and he has achieved one of power and full authority.

Place is now summarily noted by intimation and implication to serve as a background for the image of sleep. Renoir has treated his landscape as curtly as Byron began one of the cantos of *Don Juan*, 'Hail, muse etc., we left Juan sleeping.' In other words, Renoir differentiated between the devices of pictorial rhetoric and the real topic of conversation, about which he had a great deal to say.

The miracle of this painting is that even though Renoir has kept intact the tradition of decorating porcelain, he has left it far behind in this achievement. By simple reason of the care with which the figure is rendered, and the same care with which the scale of the real anatomy has been adjusted to achieve the scale of the painted anatomy, Renoir has made the image one purely of painting and not merely the representation of nature. Were this woman real, her shape would seem preposterously elongated, her neck heavy, and her breasts set impossibly far apart. But this is precisely the point: this is not a real woman but a carefully composed painted image whose subject is woman.

72

73 Claude and Renée, 1904

31 × 25 inches

Lent by the National Gallery of Canada, Ottawa

Renée holds the infant Claude in her arms. She wears a striped dress with an apron, her hair piled back upon her head. Young Claude is clad in a high-yoked dress with a wide collar, high shoes, and a ruffled hat with a large bow, of a sort of which Renoir was especially fond. The pair are placed in no specific setting with only a plain background to set off the half-length nurse who holds the little boy.

Technically the painter has used careful strokes of paint laid on top of his preliminary washes, but they are smoothly integrated so that the rendering of the forms is smooth; without any trace, however, of slickness. There is, to be sure, a sense of light in the picture, but careful examination indicates that the light is more theoretical and schematic than strictly observed, although the rendering is based on observation. But it is also based upon an awareness of the rendering of form in Italian fresco painting and at Pompeii, that is, the convention by which the roundness of forms is achieved through heightening in white or otherwise lightening the colors of the forms at their centers. In this picture there is actually a synthesis of the two methods, with the result that the figures seem heroic in quality although still based upon observed facts.

Renoir here is at the moment at which he had reached the beginnings of the *détente* from which his final style emerges. There is a relaxing of the sharpest forms into a soft-edged but by no means blurred quality. The one factor of this moment in the painter's career is that the very smoothness of the manner becomes a sort of emptiness in the less well-composed pictures. This is emphatically not the case with the picture in question here, for the final effect is not only of elegant simplicity but also of breadth and ultimate nobility of concept.

73

74 Bather, 1905

$38\frac{1}{4} \times 28\frac{3}{4}$ inches

Lent by Mr and Mrs R. Meyer de Schauensee, Devon, Pennsylvania

Here Renoir has taken his model and made her into a monumental image, but not one un-believable as a real human being. She is heroic in conception, but not impossible. The gesture is the simple one of a leg being rubbed with a bath sheet while at the same time the young woman lifts her heavy, long hair. Her face is rendered with even traces of linearity left in the presentation and a clarity of focus slightly different than that of the rest of the figure.

There is really no sense of locale indicated, for the only visible property is the elegant hat just behind the sitter on the left. This functions as a reference point, but that is all. Essentially the figure is the picture, and it is a study of interlocked and related forms and shapes, all rendered in soft reds and ochres. Already the paint touches anticipate those of the very last style, but they are not broken into shimmering separated patches of color which simulate light. They still are integrated and express a sense of a completely smooth series of forms. These latter are combined to present the sense of a great, ample, breadth of concept.

The lack of a positive sense of space is compensated by a sense of relief sculpture. In this any space is shallow and so related to the sense of the surface plane on which the picture is created. The combination of color, form, and light is one of the painter's most successful, and the result is a magnificent picture. It is so magnificent that one barely realizes how simple it is.

74

Judgement of Paris, 1908

$28\frac{3}{4} \times 36\frac{1}{4}$ inches

Lent from the Henry P. McIlhenny Collection, Philadelphia

This is one of the later masterpieces in which the aged painter achieved something very close in spirit – and just possibly in fact, as well – to the reliefs of late antiquity. By now Renoir's forms are motivated by his identification of what he saw in his models with what he knew of antique and Renaissance sculpture as well. His sense of three-dimensional space has become less insistent and has been transformed into an almost purely ornamental treatment of the surface of the picture. It is not that Venus, Juno, and Athena do not exist in space, or Paris and Mercury, either. The space is actually quite precisely described in the drawing, and the space of the landscape is actually quite generous, with the little temple set in to define the far distance. But it is the paradox of the painter's last style that represented space merges with the ornamentation of the painted surface so that the beholder is reminded once more and more strongly than ever that the painter is decorating a flat surface. Further, the emphasis on heroic forms, with concomitant departures from ordinary reality, combine to reinforce the sense and awareness of heroic shapes and bulks.

What one sees in this (and other major late works of this caliber) is Renoir's own personal, final stylistic evolution. The style itself is so personal that one has to stop to recall obvious sources: Boucher, Veronese, and Pompeiian wall paintings as well as recollections of Rubens and, more surprisingly, unless one recalls the austerity of the color, Velázquez, too. The memory of Titian's example is present, too.

What, then, keeps these last works from being mere pastiches? It is the artist's stern insistence upon the primary concerns of the painter: form, color, space, and, most crucially, the emphasis always upon the flatness of the painted surface itself.

75

76 Jean in Hunting Costume, 1910

$63\frac{1}{2} \times 38$ inches

Lent by a Private Collector

Jean stands smartly, dressed in knickers and a Norfolk jacket, one hand at his waist, his gun firmly grasped in the other. A landscape is laid up the canvas behind him, with the hills at the horizon a quarter of the way from the top. A dog lies behind Jean's feet. The tonality is prevailingly of red and gold ochres, with accents in raw umber, dull blue, what seems to be earth green, white, and Naples yellow. It is the last hue which sets the glow of the picture. There is an obvious resemblance to some of the great royal hunting portraits by Velázquez, but before that moment the memory was preconscious. Renoir never stopped looking and never stopped seeing. He remembered what he saw, and as he always looked with precise understanding at phenomena related to the painter's problems: these images became part of his store of raw material which affected his reactions to new problems. Renoir looked at his subjects in terms of painting them, but the terms always included as part of his vision preconscious recollections which only seldom became conscious quotations.

It is always necessary to remember that when Renoir painted a portrait his methods and reactions were not quite the same as when he did his bathers. In the portraits the forms remain and do not merge with the surface.

77 Self-portrait, 1910

$16\frac{1}{2} \times 13$ inches

Lent by Durand-Ruel, Paris

Here one has the marked contrast between this, the last self-portrait, and the early one in Williamstown (No. 19). The means now are of the simplest and most austere: thin washes of green, umbers, and two kinds of red. The schematic design of the picture is dazzling in the extreme, and when it is realized that it is a picture (unlike the earlier one) almost without impasto, the miracle of its achievement is the more awe-inspiring.

For what this, the most gracious and occasionally joyous master of the nineteenth century has done, by simply rendering the facts of old age and decrepitude, is to present a work of the utmost pathos to the beholder. Yet in no way is it a work to arouse pity, for Renoir did not pity himself. Discipine, determination, and even fury could prevent that. But what is achieved through the simplest of means (and in terms both of a classic Impressionist as well as a decorator of porcelains) is an image of old age which matches the late self-portraits of Titian and Rembrandt for nobility, simplicity, and eloquence of expression.

77

78 Paul Durand-Ruel, 1910

$25\frac{5}{8} \times 21\frac{1}{4}$ inches

Lent by Durand-Ruel, Paris

In this picture one sees a chair similar to that occupied by Madame Clapisson (No. 45) years earlier. But with the knowledge of a life-time, the chair is reduced to a golden-red triangle on which but a touch of black and gold guimpe is visible. The unyielding form of a black jacket – or is it a frock coat? – has been subdued into a pattern of black shot by touches of umber and reds. The hand and the cuff, though perfectly outlined, are rendered mostly as flat patterns in spite of the modelling. The background is barely suggested in its field of gold, umber, yellow, and rose touches.

Then one discovers Renoir has wrought his miracle, for he has carefully, lovingly rendered the head in all its parts, noted affectionately the double chin, the shrunken throat as it is placed within the bat-wing collar which dominates the bow-tie. The characteristics of the hair of an aged man are delineated, the set and tone of eyes. And it is in the careful organization of the two-dimensional pattern as well as in the careful rendering of the head and collar which combine to make the viewer believe the truth of the likeness, even as he admires the ornamented surface of the canvas.

78

79 Madame Renoir, 1910

$32 \times 25\frac{5}{8}$ inches

Lent by the Wadsworth Atheneum, Hartford, Connecticut. The Ella Gallup Sumner and Mary Catlin Sumner Collection

Renoir has painted Aline affectionately but unsentimentally towards the end of her life. He has set her upon a barely visible chair, rested her arm upon a cloth-covered table, indicated in Renaissance fashion a window high behind her (or perhaps it is a picture), to concentrate his attention upon her familiar features which are still lively, even lovely, in her old age. Her hair is piled high on her head with loose wisps flying, and she is wearing a loose, beltless gown, of which the sole ornaments are the embroidered collar and cuffs and the jewelled pin at the V of the neck. She looks out amiably at her viewer (actually her husband), perfectly at her ease. The miracle by which Renoir has rendered her face with its substantial traces of beauty and sense of a warm presence is accomplished by the simplicity and economy with which he has painted the form and details of her head and neck: the chin, neck, mouth, and nose are firmly indicated, only to be subordinated to the intensity of Mme Renoir's glance and the beauty of her eyes. (It is in this picture that one notices a remarkable resemblance to the features of Jean (No. 69), though the angle of the pose and the years are different.)

The calm serenity and sense of absolute security is exquisitely echoed in the form of her young puppy, Bob, cuddled in her lap. The puppy is also affectionately drawn, and its youth and helplessness contrast with the competent, serene, and gracious presence of Aline Renoir. The genuine sense of nobility and acceptance of things without complaint here curiously evoke another portrait of old age, which Renoir knew well, Tintoretto's *Self-portrait* in the Louvre. Both pictures tarry at the same level of concept and experience. It is the suggested recollection of the great Venetian picture which reinforces one's feeling that this picture is really the last great portrait of the Renaissance, three and a half centuries late.

79

80   Frau Thurneyssen and her Daughter, 1910

$39\frac{3}{8} \times 31\frac{1}{2}$ inches

Lent by the Albright-Knox Art Gallery, Buffalo, New York

A rich Bavarian commissioned Renoir to paint his wife. Renoir went to Munich where he was met with fanfare and treated splendidly. His reaction was predictable, and ever a professional, he produced one of his most appealing late portraits. Frau Thurneyssen is seated with her infant daughter upon her lap, both in most informal dress. The chair is loosely indicated, as is a flowered curtain behind them. The breadth of the rendering is notable, and this painting shows the technique of Renoir's manner most clearly.

Renoir seems to have laid in the first tones in the thinnest of washes, the paint much diluted with turpentine. On to these vague veils of color he then added more touches, these in much thicker and, therefore, more opaque paint. These touches were worked together in closely related values, and from these delicate touches, the whole picture emerged. While the composition is simple enough, with Frau Thurneyssen placed on a diagonal to the picture plane, the picture, in fact, is treated as a monumental relief. The patterns of the relief-like form which describe three-dimensional reality are broken into broad areas of rich colors, and these areas are differentiated in texture as well as hue. Renoir has directed his focus, and his viewer's as well, upon the woman's hair and eyes and on the intense, dark eyes of the little girl. The forms are all clearly indicated, but Renoir has now re-emphasized his own interest in flat, relief-like decoration.

The painting is enormously not only appealing as a decoration but also as a likeness of a woman and her small daughter. It is also fascinating to observe how much the character of the picture accords with fashionable German and Austrian decorative taste of the same period.

80

81 Alexander Thurneyssen as a Shepherd, 1911

$29\frac{5}{8} \times 36\frac{5}{8}$ inches

Lent by the Museum of Art, Rhode Island School of Design, Providence

In 1911 the Thurneyssen family sent their son, Alexander, to visit Renoir for his portrait, as the painter was rather too frail to go to Munich again to paint him. In this work, one of the riper products in the master's late manner, the young German is seen set against a landscape (this time with a much lower horizon line than usual, which increases the bulk and monumentality of the figure). His pose is quoted from an antique river god, from Michelangelo, and ultimately, from the so-called Theseus of the Parthenon. He is clad in a sheepskin and in a hat frequently worn by Gabrielle. The young man is at ease, a wooden flute rested lightly against his left thigh, while a bird is fluttering at his right hand along with two other birds. The most conspicuous thing about the portrait is the inherently curious notion of presenting an elegant young Bavarian in such surprising fancy dress. On the other hand the drawing and rendering of the body and flesh, though it is full and glows in the rosy last manner, is brilliantly solid, and the spatial structure is firmly achieved. The landscape and flower touches are rendered in delicate dabs of yellow, rose, green, and blue, and the viewer has an intense impression of an imaginary Arcadia with the young Orpheus at his ease.

As it happened, the portrait was considered an excellent likeness, and one is informed that young Thurneyssen was exceedingly proud of his high color and his auburn hair which he consistently wore as full and long as Renoir has indicated it. (The effect must have been conspicuous even in pre-war Munich.)*

The final impression of the painting, after the initial impact of a kind of inherent silliness, is that it is a beautifully realized, poetic piece, a revived version of a Renaissance decoration for a Venetian house. Renoir has deliberately painted something which was a modern version of the Renaissance *poesie*, and he has done it in the finest display of his late technical finesse. The picture is smaller than one expects it to be, truly heroic in its pictorial idiom. The viewer is left with the curious feeling that the picture would be more persuasive as a miniature or a bit of furniture ornamentation.

* Alfred Neumeyer remembers Thurneyssen, and many years later he recognized him in this portrait.

81

82   Plate Design, 1915

8¾ inches, diameter

Lent by a Private Collector

Renoir painted this to show Jean (who had taken up pottery for therapeutic reasons, on being invalided out of the army), how to decorate a plate. In this quickly brushed-in design in somber colors – almost non-color – Renoir has remembered his early vocation and has demonstrated how plates were conceived in the Second Empire. His technique in this case is that of a painter in oil, but the concept is one of the painter on porcelain. While the paint touches themselves are completely conceived and done within the limitations of the oil medium and do not in the least look like china painting, the effect, all the same, is of painting on porcelain. What Renoir did was to paint from memory a portrait of a decorated china plate.

It is this portrait quality which makes this little disc far more than an artifact or bit of memorabilia. It is in itself a complete painting, and it could very well have been snatched from an earlier painting by Renoir, perhaps a bit of decoration in a cupboard. The result is doubly fascinating for its layers of meaning. First, there is the concept of the decoration of a plate, not only how a master decorator would do it, but how a great painter would do it. Second, there is the fact that the object is, in its terms, done from memory and, by its medium, at second hand. Third, its method is that which reproduces the appearance of something simplified, reordered, and seen from a distance, in time. Last, there is the didactic aspect which demonstrates not only Renoir's professional expertise in two related fields, but also his capacity to encapsulate his knowledge of both.

This, the simplest picture in the exhibition, is in some ways the most revealing, for it shows how Renoir's creative process functioned, his concept of touches in the painting, and above all, his awareness of the function of decoration on a flat surface.

 82

83 Kneeling Woman (fresco), 1916

$8\frac{1}{2} \times 7\frac{1}{2}$ inches

Lent by a Private Collector

This precious fragment is one of the sole surviving attempts of the painter to work in the difficult and austere medium of fresco. His handling is entirely idiomatic. The work has some of the qualities of very early Italian wall paintings in its reminiscence of late antique illusionism filtered through the remnants of the Byzantine style. One is also reminded a bit of Cavallini, although the most obvious memory comes from Pompeiian wall paintings. One sees Renoir actually adapting himself to the difficult and somewhat alien technique of the frescoist. The method of painting in watercolor upon wet plaster permits really no erasures and requires absolute sureness of concept. The traditional method is to use carefully prepared cartoons from which a day's labor is planned. What Renoir has done really is to improvise within the technique, no easy task, and within the framework of the technique, one sees not only his extreme traditionalism but also his genuine archaisms: the simplifications of form, their breadth, and, most important, the use of heightening in lime white to achieve an antique formal concept. It is true that as Renoir considered the past, especially in his last years, he adopted methods which very much reflect ancient modes, so that the method and its discipline were not alien. But what he had absorbed from reading Cennino Cennini was not so much a feeling for fresco technique as a feeling for the discipline of painting in egg tempera or gouache, that is *fresco secco*.

The importance of this fragment lies in what it tells of the painter's attitude, his evocations of antiquity, his reactions to past masters and media, his feeling for a basic, ultimate norm for European pictorial expression. The bit might have come from an ancient manuscript, and it is not too far from the idiom of Fayûm paintings or Coptic textiles.

In 1877 Renoir experimented with a patented medium called MacLeish's cement (D230-3). These works are totally different in style although the frescoist's discipline is apparent.

83

84 Seated Nude, 1916

$32\frac{1}{8} \times 26\frac{5}{8}$ inches

The Art Institute of Chicago. Gift of Annie Swan Coburn to the Mr and Mrs Lewis L. Coburn Memorial Collection

This superb canvas of 1916 exemplifies the virtues and the slightly curious limitations of the painter's latest works. The limitations are those of the very virtues, for the aim of the picture is so thoroughly the creation of a noble image that its reality is slightly disturbing. It is disturbing by being so completely realistic, but the figures themselves, if conceived as representations of natural beings, are arbitrary and somewhat unappealing. The actual glow of the flesh, so glorious in the picture, is a bit too phosphorescent-seeming to be altogether reassuring, and one can be most upset by the distortion in the drawing of the main figure which gives a completely dislocated neck.

The enormous virtues of the picture lie in both its splendor and its simplicity. The design of the surface works with the implied three-dimensional structure. The colors, now applied in tiny touches and broad washes, are reduced to blue, green, black, rose ochre (with a few crimson lake touches), raw and burnt umber, and, most significant for setting a tonality, Naples yellow. It is a perfect painting in which to see and understand the fundamental and simple-minded difference between the beauty of the picture and the beauty, or lack of it, in the subject portrayed. It is also a perfect case in which to discover the dissolution of the representation of believable, perceptible three-dimensional space for the sake of the ornamentation of the surface. The distant women bathers are reduced essentially to tiny ideograms set directly beside the majestic principal subject.

It is also a perfect picture in which to see the pursuit of an Arcadian ideal and find it viable. The subject, probably Madeleine Bruno, is recognizable both for herself and as a typical invention of Renoir's with a quite recognizable style of coiffure from the time of the First World War. It is this odd combination of the perfectly familiar and plausible in an implausible context which gives the picture its distrubing overtones. One is not quite sure whether this is a highly stylized picture of a real woman or a thoroughly naturalistic picture of an imaginary woman. It is this continuing ambiguity which keeps alive the mystery and magic of these great last pictures.

84

85 Madeleine Bruno (The Bathers), 1916

$36\frac{1}{4} \times 28\frac{3}{4}$ inches

Lent by Durand-Ruel, Paris

This painting is a more satisfactory work than the immediately preceding canvas. The lines of the tree trunk echo that of Madeleine's arm, and the patterns of foliage repeat not only the forms of her torso and musculature but also echo, in the shimmering patterns of the leaves, the shimmering surface of her skin. The enormous scale of the figure comes off better in this picture, and the eccentricities of the drawing, to adjust the pattern of the human form to the exigencies of design, are more successful in this case.

It is curious to see how Renoir has here permitted himself to render an awareness of the volume of space which exists between the two figures of the picture. It is also a case in which he is accomplishing the same things which occur in Titian, but completely within his own terms. The real resemblance to Titian occurs in the method by which he has applied his paint, in flat and liquid dabs flowed on to the canvas surface to establish patches of light to describe the surface of the forms described. By this time Renoir allowed himself the luxury of making his models look to be members of the same family. This is because he very early established his own quite personal canon of female beauty with its apple-shaped cheeks and almond eyes.

Partly, of course, Renoir by now was painting away the truth of his physical infirmities to make his own personal reality. But Renoir patently was so secure that there was never any question of his merely asserting his ego for the sake of satisfaction, which lay quite simply and easily in the pact of painting. It is this intense professionalism which makes him so satisfying a painter; in this instance no other word quite does. In a world gone gaga, Renoir has remained sane, wise, and infinitely aware.

85

86 Ambroise Vollard Dressed as a Toreador, 1917

$40\frac{1}{4} \times 32\frac{3}{4}$ inches

Lent from the Collection of Mr and Mrs B. E. Bensinger, Chicago

This work sees the aged almost completely crippled painter making use of a device of half-a-century earlier: the figure in fancy dress. The painter's last dealer and friend is in the costume of a bullfighter, seated, in repose, upon a rattan chaise longue, with the fighter's cape placed behind him. The setting, which is mostly undefined, seems to include a carved stone lintel which is part of a wall made of colossal blocks of stone with a deeply incised string course. The ground merges into an undefined background at the viewer's left.

But where the Otterlo *Clown* (No. 5) is defined as existing in real space in a real place, Vollard is treated as a piece of monumental sculpture, a fragment as it were, of a great pedimental decoration. To this end, the drawing is not so much simplified, for that in the hands is precisely articulated and so also in the face, as it is changed to conform with a sense of vast bulk and mass. The head is made slightly smaller than life-size, with the result that the features seem even more concentrated than they do in photographs of Vollard. In a slight departure from his usual late stylistic handling, Renoir has, for both the velvet breeches and for the hose, changed the direction of the brushstrokes to be more or less parallel to that of the forms they render, whereas those of the face and hands are moved and twisted so as to give those features the fullest roundness and solidity.

As usual, the vanishing point horizon – is about a fifth of the way from the top edge of the painting, but rather than to attempt to describe space and surrounding air, Renoir has opted for the narrowest of volumes of space in which he has compressed truly monumentally scaled forms. The emphasis is upon the achievement of a spatial compression which is devised to emphasize the flatness of the picture surface upon which the lead white rendering of the silver braid glitters as a purely surface ornamentation. Thus, in essence, at the end of his career, Renoir again was thinking in the terms of a decorator of surfaces in transparent colors.

The color scheme is based upon warm earth reds, carmine, Naples yellow, intense green, greys and umbers. The actual effect is comparable to that observable in the last works of Titian, but the forms are even grander in scale, and the suppression of deep three-dimensional space into a scheme which evokes what must well have been the original effect of late Hellenistic and Roman relief sculpture.

See color plate XI

87 The Great Bathers, 1918

$43\frac{1}{4} \times 63$ inches

Lent by the Musée National du Jeu de Paume, Paris

This great canvas is Renoir's summation of his final view of painting of the nude. In it, by his very abandonment of subject matter, he has concentrated on his real subject: flesh observed in light and conceived as monumental sculpture. If one looks carefully, one can see that the women do indeed have clothing, and the hats do suggest clothing from the dreadful last moments of the First World War. The women in the distance not only recall Domenichino and Boucher, but also Manet in the 1860's. One also notices the flowers, the grass, the quality of the trees and the presence of the mountains and the sky. One also sees that the forms represented have been neatly and carefully adjusted to accord with the ordered scheme of the painting itself. There is a further contrast between the colors and textures of flesh and rock, foliage and clouds, and while some of the forms repeat each other – as they do in Palma Vecchio – so that the forms of the breasts and the folds of the flesh repeat those of the clouds and the mountains to achieve a pictorial metaphor in Arthur Pope's expressive phrase, "sensuous nearness and logical farness," and ultimately achieve a noble ornamentation of the whole of the pictorial surface. (It is well to remember that by the time Renoir painted this work, analytical Cubism had come and been transformed.) Because Renoir always used conventional pictorial rhetoric, it is sometimes hard to realize just how far he has departed from ordinary norms, just as, occasionally, great new truths – and heresies – are couched in the most conventional language.

The poetry here lies not only in the imagery and in the evocations of several layers of reality simultaneously, but also in the actual technique by which the aged master worked his magic. The touches are magical in their descriptive capacities and power to achieve his ends. It is these same touches, which he first learned to make in the porcelain decorator's atelier so long before, which had become means to a great end.

87

88   The Concert, 1919

$29\frac{3}{4} \times 36\frac{1}{2}$ inches

Lent by the Art Gallery of Ontario, Toronto. Gift of Reuben Wells Leonard Estate, 1954

This magnificent canvas comes from the last months of the painter's life. In it he returns to the exotic costume seen in *The Woman in Algerian Dress* of almost half a century earlier as well as to the motif of the woman *déshabillée*. In the background is a gilt table in the Louis XVI taste of the end of the nineteenth century, still to be seen at Les Collettes. On this table is a greenish blue vase filled with enormous, old-fashioned roses. Renoir's taste for plump women is now transfigured at the end into a taste for monumental imagery which seems fifth-century Greek in nobility of concept. Yet he has rendered the skin with the same care in presentation as he did for *Mme Clapisson*, albeit he has transformed their skin into an ideal concept of skin, even as he has altered and changed anatomical relationships to suit his purposes. Spatially the structure of the picture is essentially improbable, indeed, downright impossible. The rear woman's head is as dislocated as that of the *Seated Nude* (No. 84), and is so rendered for the same reason, that is, to reinforce the pictorial pattern.

The painting is done in thin washes of the artist's favorite colors. The red ochre and vermilion is now deeply tinged with burnt and raw umber, so that the sole bright reds are touches of crimson in the flowers on the figures. Most of the painting is done in thin, rubbed-in washes and veils of color. The impasto is delicately built up, and at its richest, it is, for Renoir, rather sparse. The whole is organized into a pattern of small and large forms on the surface, and simple, large and textured forms in space.

This picture is Renoir's parallel (even more than the great, late nudes are) of the *Nymph and Shepherd* by Titian in Vienna. The transformation of Renoir's style from his youth to his extreme old age is closely analogous to that of Titian. And this painting sums up Renoir's understanding of the grand manner and the noble style, and the painter ended his career on a note (in the original and classic sense) of Epicurean serenity.

See color plate XII

88

89 Flowers, probably 1919

$18\frac{1}{8} \times 16\frac{1}{4}$ inches

The Art Institute of Chicago. Gift of Joseph Winterbotham

This canvas from, apparently, the last year of Renoir's life, is typical of the work done when he had had a great roll of canvas set up on a drum, from which he could work on a number of things at the same time. One sees the same (or very similar) vase from No. 87, here also filled with roses. The piece is freely brushed on to the canvas, and the technique is one which makes full uses of washes of thin color, *essence*, paint so diluted with a mixture of turpentine that it goes on like water color. Into these wet passages he has, quite quickly, laid in his thicker touches with more oil in the paint to describe the forms of the flowers as well as that of the vase. Only when one recalls the painter's enormous physical handicaps from arthritis, and the pain which each movement cost him, that one realizes that what seems done at breakneck speed was, in fact, done slowly and deliberately. The result is that Renoir could proceed without redoing and reworking so the result really does preserve the spontaneity of his re-action to his much loved flowers.

The painting is a kind of fragment. It is interesting to see that Renoir, even at the very end, built up these fragments into relatively complete compositions, with a clear realization of the forms he was painting. His touch is still delicate and under absolute control. (This latter is awe-inspiring indeed when one recalls what his son tells of the physical effort for him involved in the act of painting.)

By this time the colors are red earth with a few crimson touches, green, raw umber, and Naples yellow, and white, though most of the white is the white of the ground of the canvas. In the very sketchiness of the technique there shines through, nonetheless, the discipline of a life time. The fact that painting porcelain permits no reworking stood Renoir well when his physique had failed him.

89

Memorabilia

90   Pair of Gloves, Camp Stool, and Bilboquet, formerly the painter's

Lent by a Private Collector

Photomicrographs of parts of the "R" (above) and "n" (facing page) of signature on *Madame Clapisson* at 5 magnifications.

Technical Note

In preparation for this exhibition, many paintings by Renoir in the collection of the Art Institute were treated in the conservation laboratory. During this process, nine of the paintings were sampled in order to ascertain what pigments and technique had been used. For this purpose invisible samples were taken, as small as 1/1000 of an inch, from each principal color tone in a painting. These totaled about ten samples a painting. The pigments were studied and identified using a polarizing microscope at magnifications up to about 1200×. In a few cases, pigment identifications were checked with an electron microprobe. Renoir's technique of applying the paint to canvas was studied by viewing the surface of each painting using a stereo microscope at magnifications up to 25×. Cross sections were not taken from the paintings to study order of layers because the nature of his technique would have rendered them relatively uninformative. Renoir rarely painted one area of paint over another; he more often applied one color next to another, and mixed them, wet paint into wet paint, on the surface of the canvas to obtain the effect he sought. The photomicrographs of the signature from *Madame Clapisson* illustrate this technique of painting wet into wet.

From this sampling it was learned that Renoir used the following palette:
lead white (basic lead carbonate) $2PbCO_3 \cdot Pb(OH)_2$
chrome yellow (lead chromate) $PbCrO_4$
Naples yellow (lead antimonate) $Pb_3(SbO_4)_2$
iron oxide yellow earth (hydrated iron oxide) $Fe_2O_3 \cdot H_2O$
red lead (red tetroxide of lead) Pb_3O_4
vermilion (mercuric sulfide) HgS
crimson lake (unidentified organic dye)
emerald green (copper aceto-arsenite) $Cu(C_2H_3O_2)_2 \cdot 3Cu(AsO_2)_2$
viridian (hydrous oxide of chromium) $Cr_2O_3 \cdot 2H_2O$
malachite (basic copper carbonate) $CuCO_3 \cdot Cu(OH)_2$
cobalt blue (cobalt aluminate) $CoO \cdot Al_2O_3$
ultramarine (sulfur containing sodium aluminium silicate) $Na_{6-10}Al_6Si_6O_{24}S_{2-4}$
bone black $C + Ca_3(PO_4)_2$

(The crimson colored lake present in many samples could not be firmly identified with the polarizing microscope due to its organic nature. Firm identification would require larger samples than were available so that the chemical compound could be ascertained by infraredspectrometry. In Renoir's own writing about his palette[1], he referred to "lac de garance" or "madder lake"; however, the descriptive term, crimson lake, is being used here in the absence of concrete proof.)

Table I lists the pigments which were found in each of the ten paintings samples; several patterns emerge. The pigments which Renoir used most often were lead white, Naples yellow, vermilion, crimson lake, and cobalt blue. Usually he used either emerald green or viridian in a particular painting; only in *Lady At The Piano* were both used in the same painting, actually mixed together for some of the green tones. Similarly he used chrome yellow, in his early paintings *Alfred Sisley* and *Lady At The Piano*, and then used Naples yellow in the remaining eight later paintings. Iron oxide yellow was found in only the three later paintings, used in addition to Naples yellow. Black was found only in a dark red tone of *Lady At The Piano*, and in a brown tone of the late *Flowers*. Malachite and red lead may have been used as experiments; each appears once in one tone in a painting. Malachite was used with lead white and Naples yellow in a few clusters of light green leaves in *Chrysanthemums*. Red lead was found, mixed with vermilion, in the bright orange-red accents in the left foreground carpet on *Lady At The Piano*. Ultramarine was found in only two paintings, *On The Terrace* and *Child In White*. In both instances the ultramarine particles were mixed with cobalt blue. The ultramarine's presence was verified by electron microprobe. A medium-toned Naples yellow was usually found in samples, however *Chrysanthemums* had a dark yellow-toned form of the pigment used alone in its medium yellows and a pale yellow-toned form used alone in its pale yellows.

Renoir most commonly used a single pigment or two pigments for a given tone. Less often did he mix more than two pigments together. Thirty-two of the samples taken, about one third, contain just one pigment. These often are brilliant colors, for example, cobalt blue in the bright blue yarn of *On The Terrace*, vermilion in the orange-red fruit of *Fruits Of The Midi*, chrome yellow in the chair post of *Alfred Sisley*, and Naples yellow in the yellow tones of *Chyrsanthemums*.

[1] *Renoir*, loan exhibition at Wildenstein and Company, New York, 1969.

Table 1 Pigments used in paintings by Renoir

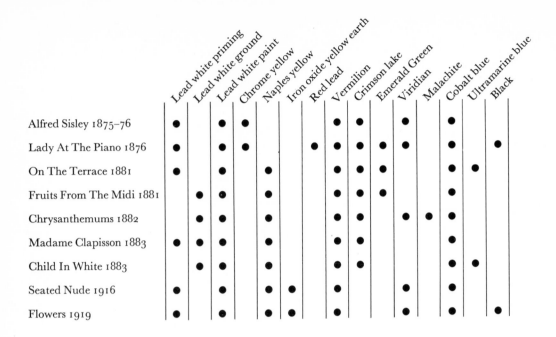

	Lead white priming	Lead white ground	Lead white paint	Chrome yellow	Naples yellow	Iron oxide yellow earth	Red lead	Vermilion	Crimson lake	Emerald Green	Viridian	Malachite	Cobalt blue	Ultramarine blue	Black
Alfred Sisley 1875–76	●	●	●					●	●	●			●		
Lady At The Piano 1876	●	●	●			●	●	●	●	●			●		●
On The Terrace 1881	●	●		●			●	●	●				●	●	
Fruits From The Midi 1881		●	●	●			●	●	●				●		
Chrysanthemums 1882		●	●	●			●	●		●	●		●		
Madame Clapisson 1883	●	●	●	●			●	●					●		
Child In White 1883		●	●	●			●	●					●	●	
Seated Nude 1916	●		●	●	●		●			●			●		
Flowers 1919	●		●	●	●		●			●			●		●

Forty-five samples contain two pigments. Examples of these include the greens of the foliage in *On the Terrace* where the yellow-greens consist of Naples yellow and cobalt blue, and dark greens are emerald green with cobalt blue. Often one of the two pigments in such a pair will be white, used to pale and lighten a tone, as in the blonde hair of *Child In White* which is lead white with Naples yellow. In *Madame Clapisson* the pinks of the background are flakes of crimson lake in lead white and the red of the chair is vermilion in lead white.

The remaining twenty-seven samples contain three or more pigments and are likely to be softer, duller tones such as the brown in *Flowers*, the distant blue sky of *On The Terrace*, or the dark tone of the piano in *Lady At The Piano*.

As Table I indicates, based on this investigation Renoir usually painted either on linen pre-primed with lead white paint or on unprimed linen to which a lead white ground had been applied. The one exception to this among the paintings sampled is *Madame Clapisson* which has a ground applied to a pre-primed linen support. According to his son, Jean,[2] Renoir liked his canvases to be reprimed with an added coat of lead white ground material. The lead white of both the priming and ground layers has particles which range from 1–10 μm, much larger than the 1–2 μm range found, usually, in the lead white used in the design layers.

The samples indicate that Renoir used a variety of materials in his flesh tones. In *Seated Nude*, light flesh tones consist of 90% lead white and 10% vermilion in 1–2 μm particles, while dark flesh tones are 90% vermilion in much larger, 2–10 μm, particles and 10% lead white. In *Madame Clapisson*, the flesh tones are again lead white and vermilion, with the addition of Naples yellow. The light flesh tones of *Child In White*

[2] Jean Renoir, *Renoir, my father*, (tr. R. and D. Weaver) Boston, 1958, p. 387

Table II Renoir *On the Terrace*

	Samples	Location in meters	Pigments	Particle size range in micrometers*	Estimated percent (volume)
1	Priming	h.0.001 w.0.192	lead white	1–4	100
2	White, child's dress	h.0.012 w.0.474	lead white	1–2	100
3	Deep red, hat	h.0.347 w.0.580	crimson lake	thin film	100
4	Orange-red, hat	h.0.381 w.0.567	vermilion	1–2	80
			lead white	1–2	20
5	yellow-light, yarn	h.0.082 w.0.076	lead white	1–2	50
			Naples yellow	2–4	50
6	yellow, dark, foliage	h.0.329 w.0.586	Naples yellow	1–4	95
			vermilion	1–2	5
7	Yellow-green, foliage	h.0.513 w.0.715	Naples yellow	1–4	95
			cobalt blue	1–10	5
8	Bright green, foliage	h.0.328 w.0.712	Naples yellow	1–4	30
			emerald green	4–14	70
9	Dark green, foliage	h.0.495 w.0.704	emerald green	4–14	90
			cobalt blue	1–12	10
10	Blue, yarn	h.0.170 w.0.157	Naples yellow	2–4	5
			cobalt blue	thin films	95
11	Blue, woman's dress	h.0.396 w.0.304	Naples yellow	2–4	15
			cobalt blue	thin films	85
12	Blue-purple, woman's dress	h.0.276 w.0.279	crimson lake	thin films	50
			cobalt blue	thin films	50
13	Blue, child's dress	h.0.072 w.0.500	lead white	1–2	70
			cobalt blue	4–12	25
			ultramarine	3–6	5
14	Pale blue, sky	h.0.985 w.0.086	lead white	1–5	65
			cobalt blue	thin films	34
			ultramarine	2–4	1
15	Blue, sky	h.0.932 w.0.022	lead white	1–4	40
			Naples yellow	3–6	10
			cobalt blue	3–6 and thin films	50
16	Brown foliage	h.0.559 w.0.785	lead white	1–2	10
			Naples yellow	1–4	30
			vermilion	1–4	5
			crimson lake	thin films	30
			emerald green	6–8	10
			cobalt blue	thin films	15

* 1 micrometer (μm) = 1/25,000 inch

Renoir *On the Terrace* 33.455 after treatment

consist of the same three pigments. The dark flesh tones of this painting are quite different, with crimson lake and cobalt blue added to lead white. The use of crimson lake with lead white occurs in the flesh tones of *Lady At The Piano* and *Alfred Sisley*, as well.

Particles of cornstarch are present in a sample of viridian from *Chrysanthemums* and a sample of crimson lake from *At The Piano*. The cornstarch is readily identified with the polarizing microscope but its presence is less easily explained. It may have been an extender in the pigments or it may have been associated with the medium for some reason.

Table II lists the samples taken from *On The Terrace* with their locations, pigments, percent of each pigment present in a mixture, and range of particle sizes. This is a typical example of the character of pigment mixtures in the other paintings which were sampled. Both crimson lake and cobalt blue, when mixed with an oil medium, tend to form thin, continuous films of color. The nature of these films makes it impossible to see individual particles in a sample, hence the descriptive term, *thin films*, as used in Table II.

Finally, in studying Renoir's paintings with a stereo microscope, a difference can be seen in his technique between the earlier paintings and the late ones such as *Seated Nude*. In the early paintings, thick, rich paint was applied to the surface of the canvas, one tone was brushed into another, with much freedom, and the tones were mixed to a degree. An example is the blue gown in *Madame Clapisson* where blue, green and white tones are brushed, wet into wet, to achieve the shimmering effect of the material. In contrast, in *Seated Nude* the paint has been thinned down by adding more medium to it. A smaller brush has been used and the forms have been modeled with many more strokes, applying a variety of tones adjacent to one another, without mixing them together on the painting's surface. The flesh tones are an example of this type of modeling of form. In the blue sky and distant foliage, varying tones of thin paint appear to have been rubbed into the surface of the canvas so that they barely cover it. The result is a much more even surface and uniformity of tones than occurs in earlier paintings.

In conclusion, this study of a chronological series of nine of Renoir's paintings has shown that he used a fairly limited palette, usually five to seven pigments, to create his complex, yet subtle, color relationships. His technique of painting wet paint into wet paint indicates that he painted rapidly and surely, knowing exactly how to achieve the particular effect which he sought. The fact that he used relatively few pigments for a given tone helps to explain how he achieved the clarity and brilliance of color which are characteristic of so many of his paintings. These factors combine to help explain his skill as a painter.

Marigene H. Butler
Associate Conservator